MultiLing 2017 Workshop on Summarization and Summary Evaluation Across Source Types and Genres (MultiLing 2017)

Valencia, Spain
3 April 2017

ISBN: 978-1-5108-3867-3

Printed from e-media with permission by:

Curran Associates, Inc.
57 Morehouse Lane
Red Hook, NY 12571

Some format issues inherent in the e-media version may also appear in this print version.

Printed by Curran Associates, Inc. (2017)

For permission requests, please contact the Association for Computational Linguistics at the address below.

Association for Computational Linguistics
209 N. Eighth Street
Stroudsburg, Pennsylvania 18360

Phone: 1-570-476-8006
Fax: 1-570-476-0860

acl@aclweb.org

Additional copies of this publication are available from:

Curran Associates, Inc.
57 Morehouse Lane
Red Hook, NY 12571 USA
Phone: 845-758-0400
Fax: 845-758-2633
Email: curran@proceedings.com
Web: www.proceedings.com

MultiLing 2017

MultiLing 2017 Workshop on Summarization and Summary Evaluation Across Source Types and Genres

Proceedings of the Workshop

EACL 2017 Workshop
April 3, 2017
Valencia, Spain

Technology sponsor: SciFY PNPC (www.scify.org)

Introduction

Welcome to the MultiLing 2017 Workshop on Summarization and Summary Evaluation Across Source Types and Genres. The Workshop is a continuation of the MultiLing community effort (cf. http://multiling.iit.demokritos.gr/) on advancing the state-of-the-art related to summarization and summary evaluation over different languages, genres and settings. We elaborate on the MultiLing focus in the next paragraphs.

Multilingual summarization across genres and sources: Summarization has been receiving increasing attention during the last years. This is mostly due to the increasing volume and redundancy of available online information but also due to the user created content. Recently, more and more interest arises for methods that will be able to function on a variety of languages and across different types of content and genres (news, social media, transcripts). This topic of research is mapped to different community tasks, covering different genres and source types: Multilingual single-document summarization ; news headline generation (new task in MultiLing 2017); user-supplied comments summarization (OnForumS task); conversation transcripts summarization (CCCS Task). The spectrum of the tasks covers a variety of real settings, identifying individual requirements and intricacies, similarly to previous MultiLing endeavors.

Multilingual summary evaluation: Summary evaluation has been an open question for several years, even though there exist methods that correlate well to human judgment, when called upon to compare systems. In the multilingual setting, it is not obvious that these methods will perform equally well to the English language setting. In fact, some preliminary results have shown that several problems may arise in the multilingual setting. The same challenges arise across different source types and genres. This section of the workshop aims to cover and discuss these research problems and corresponding solutions.

The workshop will build upon the results of a set of research community tasks, as outlined below:

Single document summarization Following the pilot task of 2015, the multi-lingual single-document summarization task will be to generate a single document summary for all the given Wikipedia feature articles from one of about 40 languages provided. The provided training data will be the Single-Document Summarization Task data from MultiLing 2015. A new set of data will be generated based on additional Wikipedia feature articles. The summaries will be evaluated via automatic methods and participants will be required to perform some limited summarization evaluations.

Headline Generation The objective of the Headline Generation (HG) task is to explore some of the challenges highlighted by current state of the art approaches on creating informative headlines to news articles: non-descriptive headlines, out-of-domain training data, and generating headlines from long documents which are not well represented by the head heuristic.

Summary Evaluation This task aims to examine how well automated systems can evaluate summaries from different languages. This task takes as input the summaries generated from automatic systems and humans in the Summarization Tasks of MultiLing 2015, but also in the Single document summarization tasks of 2015 and 2017 (when the latter is completed). The output should be a grading of the summaries. Ideally, we would want the automatic evaluation to maximally correlate to human judgement, thus the evaluation will be based on correlation measurement between estimated grades and human grades.

Online Forum Summarization Further to the successful pilot of OnForumS at MultiLing 2015, we are organizing the task again in 2017 with a brand new dataset. The OnForumS task investigates how the mass of comments found on news providers web sites (e.g., The Guardian) can be summarized. We posit that a crucial initial step towards that goal is to determine what comments link to, be that either specific news snippets or comments by other users. Furthermore, a set of labels for a given link may be articulated to capture phenomena such as agreement and sentiment with respect to the comment target.

Call Centre Conversation Summarization The Call Centre Conversation Summarization (CCCS) task — run for the first time as a pilot task in 2015 — consists in automatically generating summaries of spoken conversations in the form of textual synopses that shall inform on the content of a conversation and might be used for browsing a large database of recordings. As in CCCS 2015, participants to the task shall generate abstractive summaries from conversation transcripts that inform a reader about the main events of the conversations, such as the objective of the participants and how they are met.

Please keep in mind that the above tasks will run also during and after the Workshop itself. An addendum to the proceedings, containing system reports and evaluations, will be provided in the MultiLing website (cf. http://multiling.iit.demokritos.gr/pages/view/1638/multiling-2017-proceedings-addendum) as reports become available and tasks progress.

We thank you for your contribution and participation in MultiLing 2017 and we hope that we will all enjoy this opportunity to further the summarization state-of-the-art through a productive and knowledge-rich meeting.

George Giannakopoulos

on Behalf of the MultiLing Organizers

Organizers:

George Giannakopoulos - NCSR Demokritos (General Chair, Summary Evaluation Task)
Benoit Favre - LIF (CCCS, Headline Generation Task)
Elena Lloret - University of Alicante (Headline Generation Task)
John M. Conroy - IDA Center for Computing Sciences (Single Document Summarization Task)
Josef Steinberger - University of West Bohemia (OnForumS task)
Marina Litvak - Sami Shamoon College of Engineering (Headline Generation Task)
Peter Rankel - Elder Research Inc. (Single Document Summarization Task)

Program Committee:

Udo Kruschwitz - University of Essex
Horacio Saggion - Universitat Pompeu Fabra
Katja Filippova - Google
John M. Conroy - IDA Center for Computing Sciences
Vangelis Karkaletsis - NCSR Demokritos
Laura Plaza - UNED
Francesco Ronzano - Universitat Pompeu Fabra
Mark Last - Ben-Gurion University of the Negev
George Petasis - NCSR Demokritos
Elena Lloret - University of Alicante
Ahmet Aker - Universität Duisburg-Essen
Josef Steinberger - University of West Bohemia
Benoit Favre - LIF
Marina Litvak - Sami Shamoon College of Engineering
Mijail Alexandrov Kabadjov - University of Essex
Natalia Vanetik - Sami Shamoon College of Engineering
Florian Boudin - University of Nantes
Mahmoud El-Haj - Lancaster University
George Giannakopoulos - NCSR Demokritos

Invited Speaker:

Enrique Alfonseca, Google

Table of Contents

Workshop Program

April 3rd, 2017

09:30–11:00 Opening and Invited talk

09:30–09:45 *MultiLing 2017 Welcome*
George Giannakopoulos

09:45–11:00 *Invited talk: Sentence Compression for Conversational Search*
Enrique Alfonseca, Google

11:00–11:30 Coffee break

11:30–13:00 MultiLing Tasks and Systems I

11:30–11:50 *MultiLing 2017 Overview*
George Giannakopoulos, John Conroy, Jeff Kubina, Peter A. Rankel, Elena Lloret, Josef Steinberger, Marina Litvak and Benoit Favre

11:50–12:10 *Decoupling Encoder and Decoder Networks for Abstractive Document Summarization*
Ying Xu, Jey Han Lau, Timothy Baldwin and Trevor Cohn

12:10–12:30 *Centroid-based Text Summarization through Compositionality of Word Embeddings*
Gaetano Rossiello, Pierpaolo Basile and Giovanni Semeraro

12:30–12:50 *Query-based summarization using MDL principle*
Marina Litvak and Natalia Vanetik

April 3rd, 2017 (continued)

14:30–16:00 MultiLing Tasks and Systems II

14:30–14:50 *Multilingual Single Document Summarization Overview*
John Conroy

14:50–15:10 *Word Embedding and Topic Modeling Enhanced Multiple Features for Content Linking and Argument / Sentiment Labeling in Online Forums*
Lei Li, Liyuan Mao and Moye Chen

15:10–15:30 *Ultra-Concise Multi-genre Summarisation of Web2.0: towards Intelligent Content Generation*
Elena Lloret, Ester Boldrini, Patricio Martinez-Barco and Manuel Palomar

15:30–15:50 *Machine Learning Approach to Evaluate MultiLingual Summaries*
Samira Ellouze, Maher Jaoua and Lamia Hadrich Belguith

16:00–16:30 Coffee break and poster setup

16:30–18:00 Poster session and Closing

16:30–17:30 ***Poster session***

17:30–18:00 ***Closing remarks and planning***

MultiLing 2017 Overview

George Giannakopoulos
NCSR "Demokritos", Greece

John M. Conroy
IDA / Center for Comp. Sciences, U.S.A

Jeff Kubina
U.S. Dep. of Defense, U.S.A

Peter A. Rankel
Elder Research, U.S.A

Elena Lloret
Univ. of Alicante, Spain

Josef Steinberger
Univ. of West Bohemia, Czech Republic

Marina Litvak
Shamoon College of Engineering, Israel

Benoit Favre
LIF, France

Abstract

In this brief report we present an overview of the MultiLing 2017 effort and workshop, as implemented within EACL 2017. MultiLing is a community-driven initiative that pushes the state-of-the-art in Automatic Summarization by providing data sets and fostering further research and development of summarization systems. This year the scope of the workshop was widened, bringing together researchers that work on summarization across sources, languages and genres. We summarize the main tasks planned and implemented this year, also providing insights on next steps.

1 Overview

MultiLing covers a variety of topics on Natural Language Processing, focused on the multilingual aspect of summarization:

- **Multilingual summarization across genres and sources:** Summarization has been receiving increasing attention during the last years. This is mostly due to the increasing volume and redundancy of available online information but also due to the user created content. Recently, more and more interest arises for methods that will be able to function on a variety of languages and across different types of content and genres (news, social media, transcripts).

  This topic of research is mapped to different community tasks, covering different genres and source types:

  - Multilingual single-document summarization (Giannakopoulos et al., 2015);
  - user-supplied comments summarization (OnForumS task (Kabadjov et al., 2015));
  - conversation transcripts summarization (see also (Favre et al., 2015)).

  The spectrum of the tasks covers a variety of real settings, identifying individual requirements and intricacies, similarly to previous MultiLing endeavours (Giannakopoulos et al., 2011a; Giannakopoulos, 2013; Elhadad et al., 2013; Giannakopoulos et al., 2015).

- **Multilingual summary evaluation:** Summary evaluation has been an open question for several years, even though there exist methods that correlate well to human judgement, when called upon to compare systems. In the multilingual setting, it is not obvious that these methods will perform equally well to the English language setting. In fact, some preliminary results have shown that several problems may arise in the multilingual setting (Giannakopoulos et al., 2011a). The same challenges arise across different source types and genres. This aspect of the workshop aims to cover and discuss these research problems and corresponding solutions.

The workshop builds upon the results of a set of research **community tasks**, which are elaborated on in the following paragraphs. However, this year MultiLing also hosts works beyond the tasks themselves, but still within the scope of automatic summarization and evaluation in different genres and settings.

2 Community Tasks

In this year's MultiLing community effort we are implementing the following tasks:

Proceedings of the MultiLing 2017 Workshop on Summarization and Summary Evaluation Across Source Types and Genres, pages 1–6,
Valencia, Spain, April 3, 2017.

- Multilingual Single-Document Summarization (MSS)
- Multilingual Summary Evaluation (MSE)
- Online Forum Summarization (OnForumS)
- Call Centre Conversation Summarization (CCCS)
- Headline Generation Task (HG)

Due to time limitations, all but the MSS and OnForumS tasks will run beyond the workshop timespan, thus the proceedings will be complemented by the proceedings addendum [1], containing system reports and evaluation results.

3 Multilingual Single-Document Summarization Task Overview

The Multilingual Single-document Summarization 2017 posed a task to measure the performance of multilingual, single-document, summarization systems using a dataset derived from the featured articles of 41 Wikipedias. The objective was to assess the performance of automatic summarization techniques on text documents covering a diverse range of languages and topics outside the news domain. This section describes the task, the dataset and the methods to be used to evaluate the submitted summaries. To give amble time for evaluation the results and analysis will be presented at the workshop and published later. The objective of this task, like the 2015 Multilingual Single-document Summarization Task, was to stimulate research and assess the performance of automatic single-document summarization systems on documents covering a large range of sizes, languages, and topics.

3.1 Task and Dataset Description

Each participating system of the task was to compute a summary for each document in at least one of the datasets 41 languages. To remove any potential bias in the evaluation of generated summaries that are too small, the human summary length in characters was provided for each test document and generated summaries were expected to be close to it.

[1] Cf. http://multiling.iit.demokritos.gr/pages/view/1638/multiling-2017-proceedings-addendum.

The testing dataset was created using the same steps as reported in Section 2 of (Giannakopoulos et al., 2015) and excluded the articles in the training dataset (which was the testing dataset for the task in 2015). For each language Table 1 contains the mean character size of the summary and body of the articles selected for the test dataset. Within the dataset there is no correlation between the summary and body size of the articles, in fact, the variance in the summary size is small. This is likely because Wikipedia style requirements dictate that a summary be at most four paragraphs,[2] regardless of article size, and paragraphs be reasonably sized.[3]

3.2 Preprocessing and Evaluation

For the evaluation the baseline summary for each article in the dataset was the prefix substring of the article's body text having the same length as the human summary of the article. An oracle summary was also computed for each article using the combinatorial covering algorithm in (Davis et al., 2012) by selecting sentences from its body text to cover the tokens in the human summary using as few sentences as possible until its size exceeded the human summary, upon which it was truncated.

Preprocessing of all the submitted and human summaries was performed using the Natural Language Toolkit (Bird et al., 2009). Sentence splitting was done using *punkt()*. Models based on the Wikipedia data were built for each language. For each summary the pre-processing steps were:

1. all multiple white-spaces and control characters are convert to a single space
2. any leading space is removed
3. the resulting text string is truncated to the human summary length
4. the text is tokenized and, if possible, lemmatized
5. all tokens without a letter or number are discarded
6. all remaining tokens are lowercased.

[2] https://en.wikipedia.org/wiki/Wikipedia:LEAD

[3] https://en.wikipedia.org/wiki/Wikipedia:WBA

Table 1: Dataset Languages and Sizes

ISO	LANGUAGE	SUMMARY	BODY	ISO	LANGUAGE	SUMMARY	BODY
af	Afrikaans	1743 (784)	32407 (20378)	ka	Georgian	1114 (682)	23626 (23018)
ar	Arabic	2129 (1045)	38682 (16354)	ko	Korean	905 (491)	15723 (7098)
az	Azerbaijani	1375 (937)	48687 (45855)	li	Limburgish	569 (237)	14177 (16326)
bg	Bulgarian	1451 (782)	29421 (10774)	lv	Latvian	1334 (514)	25292 (13464)
bs	Bosnian	1275 (801)	26497 (15319)	mr	Marathi	970 (653)	14727 (8438)
ca	Catalan	1733 (906)	28536 (14460)	ms	Malay	1420 (952)	22820 (16851)
cs	Czech	1947 (745)	33751 (24010)	nl	Dutch	1316 (562)	36638 (18062)
de	German	1122 (470)	42838 (30382)	nn	Norwegian	965 (493)	17772 (9073)
el	Greek	1582 (905)	36081 (16652)	no	Nor.-Bok.	1808 (913)	37128 (22024)
en	English	1878 (735)	20683 (9644)	pl	Polish	1470 (687)	31460 (16319)
eo	Esperanto	1286 (875)	22905 (10279)	pt	Portuguese	2247 (759)	37189 (16777)
es	Spanish	2083 (892)	47670 (39981)	ro	Romanian	2204 (710)	38973 (20349)
eu	Basque	1105 (742)	23558 (16672)	ru	Russian	1855 (915)	59337 (27360)
fa	Persian	1850 (581)	29525 (13172)	simple	Simp. Eng.	973 (351)	9793 (7027)
fi	Finnish	1135 (406)	23971 (10538)	sk	Slovak	1104 (631)	26102 (11024)
fr	French	1924 (884)	65960 (41289)	th	Thai	1851 (951)	30549 (15203)
hr	Croatian	1398 (1119)	22430 (13583)	tr	Turkish	2059 (807)	32240 (23667)
id	Indonesian	1813 (964)	26634 (18564)	tt	Tagalog	1149 (779)	23648 (14139)
it	Italian	1743 (701)	51461 (20832)	uk	Ukrainian	1023 (758)	35552 (32014)
ja	Japanese	383 (275)	21349 (14694)	zh	Chinese	662 (245)	10614 (6338)
jv	Javanese	1118 (855)	14033 (10810)				

Table 1: The table lists the languages in the dataset with the first column containing the ISO code for each the language, the second column the name of the language, and the remaining columns containing the mean size, in characters, and standard deviation, in parentheses, of the summary and body of the article. For example, for English the mean size of the human summaries is 1,857 characters.

As of the time of publication of the proceedings, three teams have participated and automatic methods of scoring the subumissions, using ROUGE (Lin, 2004) and MeMoG (Gia,), are underway and will be presented at the EACL 2017 workshop. A human evaluation will proceed afterwards.

4 OnForumS Task

Further to the pilot of OnForumS in 2015, we organized the task again in 2017 with a brand new dataset. The OnForumS task investigates how the mass of comments found on news providers web sites can be summarized. We posit that a crucial initial step towards that goal is to determine what comments link to, be that either specific news snippets or comments by other users. Furthermore, a set of labels for a given link may be articulated to capture phenomena such as agreement and sentiment with respect to the comment target. Solving this labelled linking problem can enable recognition of salience (e.g., snippets/comments with most links) and relations between comments (e.g., agreement).

The OnForumS task is a particular specification of the linking task, in which systems take as input a news article with comments and were asked to link and label (sentiment, argument) each comment to sentences in the article, to the article topic as a whole or to other comments. The set of possible labels is for sentiment is [POS, NEUT, NEG] and the set of possible argument labels is [IN FAVOR, AGAINST, IMPARTIAL].

This year we focus on English (The Guardian) and Italian (La Repubblica) as in the previous edition and we released the 2015 test data as training data.

The 2017 text collection contains 19 English and 19 Italian articles. This year we had 4 participanting teams and together with two baselines we received 9 runs. The evaluation focuses on how many of the links and labels were correctly identified, as in the previous OnForumS run. The next step is to manually validate the links and labels using CrowdFlower.

5 MultiLingual Summary Evaluation

The summary evaluation task revisits the multilingually applicable evaluation challenge. The aim is to introduce novel, automatic evaluation methods of summary evaluation. Even though, currently, systems are evaluated using the ROUGE (Lin, 2004) and MeMoG (Gia,) metrics, there exists a big gap between automatic methods and manual annotations, especially in non-English settings (Giannakopoulos et al., 2011b).

This year's task reuses the MultiLing 2013 and 2015 single-document and multi-document summarization corpora and evalautions. Furthermore, we generate summary variations (often through inducing "noise"), which the evaluation systems will be asked to grade. These variations include:

- Sentence re-ordering;
- Random sentence replacement;
- Merging between different summaries.

All the above changes will be studied, to understand the strengths and weaknesses of different evaluation methods with respect to these synthetic deviations. Then, a human evaluation will be conducted to see whether humans respond similarly to the automatic methods with respect to the different noise types.

The aim of this task and study is to understand how variations of text change its perceived quality of a summary. It also aims to highlight the (in)sufficiency of existing methods in the multilingual setting and promote new, more robust approaches for summary evaluation.

6 Tasks in preparation

6.1 Headline Generation

The Headline Generation (HG) task aims to explore some of the challenges highlighted by current state of the art approaches on creating informative headlines to news articles: non-descriptive headlines, out-of-domain training data, and generating headlines from long documents which are not well represented by the head heuristic. This task has been previously addressed in past summarization challenges, such as the well-known Document Understanding Conferences (DUC) for the 2002, 2003 or 2004 editions.

With the high-rate of information increase, novel summarization methods that could condense and extract relevant information in just one sentence (i.e., headlines) would perfectly fit in today's society for creating better information access and processing tools. We will rerun the headline generation task in DUC[4] 2002, 2003, 2004 conditions

[4]Cf. http://duc.nist.gov//

in order to create comparable results, and determine to what extent the techniques and methods have improved with respect to former participants.

Moreover, we will encourage multilingual or cross-lingual approaches able to generate headlines for at least two languages. We expect to make available a large set of training data for headline generation, and create evaluation conditions to objectively assess and compare different approaches.

6.2 Call Centre Conversation Summarization

The Call Centre Conversation Summarization (CCCS) task — run for the first time as a pilot task in 2015 — consists in automatically generating summaries of spoken conversations in the form of textual synopses that shall inform on the content of a conversation and might be used for browsing a large database of recordings. As in CCCS 2015, participants to the task shall generate abstractive summaries from conversation transcripts that inform a reader about the main events of the conversations, such as the objective of the participants and how they are met. Evaluation will be performed by ROUGE-like measures based on human-written summaries as in CCCS 2015, and — if possible — will be coupled by manual evaluation, depending on the funding we can secure for the task.

7 Conclusion

This year MultiLing covers a number of challenging problems related to summarization. In the proceedings (and the addendum) one can find various methods using deep learning and word embeddings, topic modeling, optimization and other approaches to achieve summarization and summary evaluation across settings.

The rest of the proceedings will allow the reader to examine interesting challenges related to abstractive summarization, argument labeling, multi-genre, multi-document and query-based summarization. They will also identify and attemp to tackle important challenges related to summary evaluation beyond English.

We hope that the conclusion of the tasks after the workshop will provide the grounds for further research and open systems development, revising and improving the way summarization is modeled, faced, evaluated and implemented in the years to come.

8 Acknowledgements

This work was supported by project MediaGist, EUs FP7 People Programme (Marie Curie Actions), no. 630786, MediaGist.

References

Steven Bird, Ewan Klein, and Edward Loper. 2009. *Natural language processing with Python: analyzing text with the natural language toolkit.* " O'Reilly Media, Inc.".

Sashka T. Davis, John M. Conroy, and Judith D. Schlesinger. 2012. OCCAMS - an optimal combinatorial covering algorithm for multi-document summarization. In *12th IEEE International Conference on Data Mining Workshops, ICDM Workshops, Brussels, Belgium, December 10, 2012*, pages 454–463.

Michael Elhadad, Sabino Miranda-Jiménez, Josef Steinberger, and George Giannakopoulos. 2013. Multi-document multilingual summarization corpus preparation, part 2: Czech, hebrew and spanish. *MultiLing 2013*, page 13.

Benoit Favre, Evgeny Stepanov, Jérémy Trione, Frédéric Béchet, and Giuseppe Riccardi. 2015. Call centre conversation summarization: A pilot task at multiling 2015. In *16th Annual Meeting of the Special Interest Group on Discourse and Dialogue*, page 232.

Summarization system evaluation variations based on n-gram graphs.

George Giannakopoulos, Mahmoud El-Haj, Benoit Favre, Marina Litvak, Josef Steinberger, and Vasudeva Varma. 2011a. Tac2011 multiling pilot overview. In *TAC 2011 Workshop*.

George Giannakopoulos, Mahmoud El-Haj, Benoit Favre, Marina Litvak, Josef Steinberger, and Vasudeva Varma. 2011b. Tac2011 multiling pilot overview. In *TAC 2011 Workshop*.

George Giannakopoulos, Jeff Kubina, John M. Conroy, Josef Steinberger, Benoit Favre, Mijail Kabadjov, Udo Kruschwitz, and Massimo Poesio. 2015. Multiling 2015: Multilingual summarization of single and multi-documents, on-line fora, and call-center conversations. In *SIGDIAL 2015*.

George Giannakopoulos. 2013. Multi-document multilingual summarization and evaluation tracks in acl 2013 multiling workshop. In *Proceedings of the MultiLing 2013 Workshop on Multilingual Multi-document Summarization*, pages 20–28.

Mijail Kabadjov, Josef Steinberger, Emma Barker, Udo Kruschwitz, and Massimo Poesio. 2015. Onforums: The shared task on online forum summarisation at multiling'15. In *Proceedings of the 7th*

Forum for Information Retrieval Evaluation, pages 21–26. ACM.

Chin-Yew Lin. 2004. Rouge: A package for automatic evaluation of summaries. In *Text summarization branches out: Proceedings of the ACL-04 workshop*, volume 8. Barcelona, Spain.

Decoupling Encoder and Decoder Networks for Abstractive Document Summarization

Ying Xu[1], Jey Han Lau[2,3], Timothy Baldwin[3] and Trevor Cohn[3]

[1]Monash University
[2]IBM Research
[3]The University of Melbourne
ying.xu@monash.edu, jeyhan.lau@gmail.com
tb@ldwin.net, trevor.cohn@unimelb.edu.au

Abstract

Abstractive document summarization seeks to automatically generate a summary for a document, based on some abstract "understanding" of the original document. State-of-the-art techniques traditionally use attentive encoder–decoder architectures. However, due to the large number of parameters in these models, they require large training datasets and long training times. In this paper, we propose decoupling the encoder and decoder networks, and training them separately. We encode documents using an unsupervised document encoder, and then feed the document vector to a recurrent neural network decoder. With this decoupled architecture, we decrease the number of parameters in the decoder substantially, and shorten its training time. Experiments show that the decoupled model achieves comparable performance with state-of-the-art models for in-domain documents, but less well for out-of-domain documents.

1 Introduction

Abstractive document summarization is a challenging natural language understanding task. Abstractive methods first encode the original document into a high-level representation, and then decode it into the target summary.

Rush et al. (2015) proposed the task of headline generation as the first step towards abstractive summarization. Instead of using the full document, the authors experimented with using the first sentence as input, with the aim of generating a coherent headline given the sentence.

The current state-of-art system for the task is based on an attentive encoder and a recurrent decoder (Chopra et al., 2016), which is an extension of the methodology of Rush et al. (2015). The encoder and decoder are trained jointly, and the decoder attends to different parts of the document during generation. It has a large number of parameters, and thus requires large-scale training data and long training times.

In this paper, we propose decoupling the encoder and decoder. We encode documents using `doc2vec` (Le and Mikolov, 2014), as it has been demonstrated to be a competitive unsupervised document encoder (Lau and Baldwin, 2016). We incorporate `doc2vec` vectors of input documents to the decoder as an additional signal, to generate sentences that are not only coherent but are also related to the original documents. Compared to the standard joint encoder–decoder design, the decoupled architecture has less parameters for the decoder, and thus requires less training data and trains faster.[1] The downside of the decoupled architecture is that the `doc2vec` signal is not updated in the decoder, and its document representation could be sub-optimal for the decoder to generate good summaries. Our experiments reveal that the decoupled architecture works well in-domain, but less well out-of-domain, as a consequence of the fixed capacity of the document encoding as well as having no explicit copy mechanism.

2 Attentive Recurrent Neural Network: A Joint Encoder–decoder Architecture

The attentive recurrent neural network is composed of an attentive encoder and a recurrent decoder (Chopra et al., 2016), where the encoder is

[1]The training time is decreased from 4 days (with full GIGAWORD) for the coupled model (Rush et al., 2015) to 2 days (with 75% GIGAWORD) in our model with comparable in-domain performance.

Proceedings of the MultiLing 2017 Workshop on Summarization and Summary Evaluation Across Source Types and Genres, pages 7–11,
Valencia, Spain, April 3, 2017.

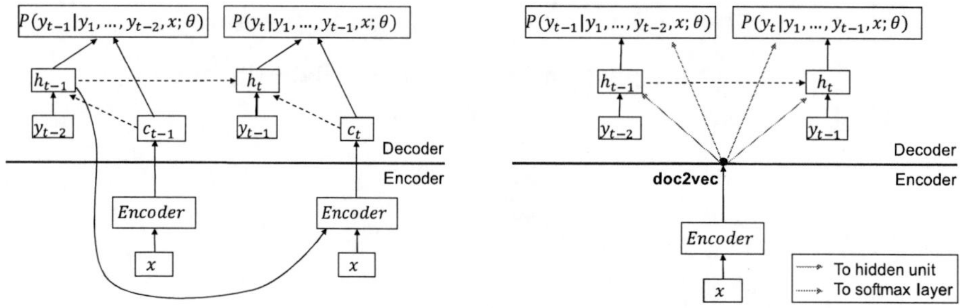

(a) Joint encoder–decoder architecture

(b) Decoupled encoder–decoder architecture

Figure 1: Encoder–decoder architectures

a fixed-window feed-forward network and the decoder is a recurrent neural network (RNN: Elman (1998), Mikolov et al. (2010)) language model and parameters from both networks are trained together. Let $\mathbf{x}$ denote the document, $\mathbf{y}$ the summary, θ the set of parameters to be learnt, and $\mathbf{y} = y_1, y_2, ..., y_N$ a word sequence of length N. When decoding, $\mathbf{y}$ is computed as $\operatorname{argmax} P(\mathbf{y}|\mathbf{x};\theta)$, where the conditional probability $P(\mathbf{y}|\mathbf{x};\theta)$ can be calculated from each word y_t in the sequence, i.e. $P(\mathbf{y}|\mathbf{x};\theta) = \prod_{t=1}^{N} P(y_t|\{y_1, ..., y_{t-1}\}, \mathbf{x}; \theta)$.

For the recurrent decoder, the conditional probability of each word is given as $P(y_t|\{y_1, ..., y_{i-1}\}, \mathbf{x}; \theta) = g_\theta(\mathbf{h}_t, \mathbf{c}_t)$, where $\mathbf{h}_t$ represents the hidden state of RNN, i.e. $\mathbf{h}_t = g_\theta(y_{t-1}, \mathbf{h}_{t-1}, \mathbf{c}_t)$, and $\mathbf{c}_t$ the output of the encoder at time t.

For the attentive encoder, $\mathbf{x}$ is computed by attending to some of the source words using the previous hidden state $\mathbf{h}_{t-1}$.[2] Figure 1a demonstrates the dependencies between the next generated word y_t and document $\mathbf{x}$, given the parameters θ.

The decoupled architecture ensures that the information from document $\mathbf{x}$ is adapted to the current context of the generated summary.

3 Decoupled Encoder–decoder Architecture for Document Summarization

A decoupled encoder–decoder architecture has a clear boundary between the encoder and decoder: it can be seen as a pipeline model where the output of the encoder is fed as an input to the decoder, so the encoder and decoder modules can be trained separately. Figure 1b illustrates how the encoder and decoder are decoupled from each other. Here, we use `doc2vec` the document encoder and a long-short term memory network (LSTM: Hochreiter and Schmidhuber (1997)) as the decoder.

`doc2vec` is an extension of `word2vec` (Mikolov et al., 2013), a popular deep learning method for learning word embeddings. In `word2vec` (based on the `skipgram` variant) the embedding of a target word is learnt by optimising it to predict its position-indexed neighbouring words. `doc2vec` (based on the `dbow` variant) is based on the same idea, except that the target word is now the document itself, and the document vector is optimised to predict the document words. Note that the `dbow` implementation does not take into account the order of the words (hence its name "distributed bag of words"). Once the model is trained, embeddings of new/unseen documents can be inferred from the pre-trained model efficiently. As an encoder, `doc2vec` is completely unsupervised, and uses no labelled information or signal from the decoder.

The decoder is an RNN language model (Mikolov et al., 2010), implemented as an LSTM (Hochreiter and Schmidhuber, 1997). Formally:

$$\begin{aligned}
\mathbf{i}_t &= W_i\mathbf{x}_t + U_i\mathbf{h}_{t-1} + \mathbf{b}_i \\
\mathbf{f}_t &= W_f\mathbf{x}_t + U_f\mathbf{h}_{t-1} + \mathbf{b}_f \\
\mathbf{o}_t &= W_o\mathbf{x}_t + U_o\mathbf{h}_{t-1} + \mathbf{b}_o \\
\mathbf{j}_t &= W_j\mathbf{x}_t + U_j\mathbf{h}_{t-1} + \mathbf{b}_j \\
\mathbf{c}_t &= \mathbf{c}_{t-1} * \sigma(\mathbf{f}_t) + \tanh(\mathbf{j}_t) * \sigma(\mathbf{i}_t) \\
\mathbf{h}_t &= \tanh(\mathbf{c}_t) * \sigma(\mathbf{o}_t)
\end{aligned} \tag{1}$$

where $\mathbf{i}_t$, $\mathbf{f}_t$ and $\mathbf{o}_t$ are input, forget and output gates, respectively; $\mathbf{j}_t$, $\mathbf{c}_t$ and $\mathbf{h}_t$ represent the new

[2]The unnormalised attention weights are computed by combining $\mathbf{h}_{t-1}$ with the convolutional embedding of each source word via dot product.

Combination	Equation
`add-input`	$\mathbf{i}'_t = \mathbf{i}_t + \mathbf{d}$
`add-hidden`	$\mathbf{h}'_t = \mathbf{h}_t + \mathbf{d}$
`stack-input`	$\mathbf{i}'_t = [\mathbf{i}_t; \mathbf{d}]$
`stack-hidden`	$\mathbf{h}'_t = [\mathbf{h}_t; \mathbf{d}]$
`mlp-input`	$\mathbf{i}'_t = \tanh(W_i \mathbf{i}_t + W_d \mathbf{d} + b)$
`mlp-hidden`	$\mathbf{h}'_t = \tanh(W_i \mathbf{h}_t + W_d \mathbf{d} + b)$

Table 1: Incorporation of `doc2vec` signal in the decoder. $\mathbf{d}$ denotes the `doc2vec` vector; $\mathbf{i}_t$ ($\mathbf{h}_t$) is the input (hidden) vector at time t; and "$[\cdot;\cdot]$" denotes vector concatenation.

input, new context and new hidden state, respectively; $*$ is the elementwise vector product; and σ is the sigmoid activation function.

Given an input word and previous hidden state, the decoder predicts the next word and generates the summary one word at a time.

To generate summaries that are related to the document, we incorporate the `doc2vec` input document signal to the decoder using several methods proposed by Hoang et al. (2016). There are two layers where we can incorporate `doc2vec`: in the input layer (`input`), or hidden layer (`hidden`). There are three methods of incorporation: addition (`add`), stacking (`stack`), or via a multilayer perceptron (`mlp`). Table 1 illustrates the 6 possible approaches to incorporation.

Note that `add` requires `doc2vec` to have the same vector dimensionality as the layer it is combined with, and `stack-hidden` doubles the hidden size (assuming they have the same dimensions), resulting in a large output projection matrix and longer training time.

4 Experiments and Results

4.1 Datasets

We test our decoupled architecture for the headline generation task. Following Chopra et al. (2016), we run experiments using GIGAWORD, DUC03 and DUC04.[3]

GIGAWORD is preprocessed according to Rush et al. (2015), yielding 4.3 million examples. For in-domain experiments, we randomly sample 2,000 examples for each validation and test set, and use the remaining examples for training. We tune hyper-parameters based on validation perplexity and evaluate performance on the test set using the ROUGE metric (Lin, 2004), following the same evaluation style of benchmark systems (Rush et al., 2015; Chopra et al., 2016). For out-of-domain experiments, we use the same models trained from GIGAWORD, but tune using DUC03 and test on DUC04; DUC03 and DUC04 each have 500 examples.

For the `doc2vec` encoder, we train using GIGAWORD and infer document vectors for validation and test examples using the trained model. Valid and test examples are excluded from the `doc2vec` training data.

4.2 Hyper-parameter tuning

For the encoder, we explore using a range of document lengths (first 20/30/40/50 words) to generate the input representation. Validation results show that using the first 20 words produces the best performance, suggesting that this length contains sufficient information to generate headlines.

We next test the 6 different ways to incorporate `doc2vec` into the decoder. We find that stacking the `doc2vec` vector with the input (`stack-input`) has the most consistent performance, while `mlp` is competitive, and `add` performs the worst. Interestingly, for `mlp` and `stack`, we find the difference between `input` and `hidden` to be small.

For the recurrent decoder, hyper-parameters that are tuned include the mini-batch size, hidden layer size, number of LSTM layers, number of training epochs, learning rate, and drop out rate. The best results is achieved with a mini-batch size of 128, hidden size of 900, and one LSTM layer. The best perplexity is obtained after 3 to 4 epochs, with a learning rate of 0.001. More training epochs are needed when we reduce the learning rate to 0.0001. For in-domain experiments, the best results are achieved with a dropout rate of 0.1, while for out-of-domain experiments, the best performance prefers a higher dropout rate at 0.4. This suggests that dropout plays an important role in combating over-fitting, and it is especially useful for out-of-domain data.

4.3 Results

We compare our model (RDS: Recurrent Decoupled Summarizer) with 4 state-of-art models: ABS, ABS+ (Rush et al., 2015); RAS-LSTM and RAS-Elman (Chopra et al., 2016), which are all joint encoder–decoder models. For in-domain results, we present ROUGE-1/2/L full-length F-scores in Table 2. For out-of-domain results we

[3]GIGAWORD: https://catalog.ldc.upenn.edu/LDC2003T05; DUC: http://duc.nist.gov/

System	ROUGE-1	ROUGE-2	ROUGE-L
ABS	29.6	11.3	26.4
ABS+	29.8	11.9	30.0
RAS-LSTM	32.6	14.7	30.0
RAS-Elman	33.8	16.0	31.2
RDS	*30.7*	*11.3*	*27.6*
RDS (75%)	29.1	10.0	26.3
RDS (50%)	27.4	8.9	24.9

Table 2: Comparison of ROUGE scores (full length F-score) for in-domain experiments.

System	ROUGE-1	ROUGE-2	ROUGE-L
Prefix	22.4	6.5	19.7
ABS	26.6	7.1	22.1
ABS+	28.2	8.5	23.8
RAS-LSTM	27.4	7.7	23.1
RAS-Elman	29.0	8.3	24.1
RDS	*16.7*	*3.7*	*14.4*

Table 3: Comparison of ROUGE scores (recall at 75 bytes) for out-of-domain experiments.

report ROUGE-1/2/L recall at 75 bytes in Table 3, where only the first 75 bytes of model-generated summary is used for evaluation against the references.

ABS employs an attentive encoder and a feed-forward neural network decoder. ABS+ works in the same way as ABS, but further tunes the decoder using Z-MERT (Zaidan, 2009). RAS-LSTM and RAS-Elman are detailed in Section 2; the only difference between them is that RAS-LSTM uses an LSTM decoder, while RAS-Elman uses a simple RNN decoder. Prefix is a baseline model where the first 75 byte of the document is used as the title.

Looking at Table 2, models with a recurrent decoder (RDS and RAS) perform better than those with a feed-forward decoder (ABS). The decoupled architecture RDS achieves competitive performance, although the fully joint RAS models achieve the best results. Chopra et al. (2016) found that RAS models perform best with a beam size of 10, while we found that RDS performs best with greedy argmax decoding.

We further experiment with training RDS using less data (50% and 75%), and find that its performance degrades slightly. Encouragingly, its ROUGE-1 is comparable to ABS when RDS is trained using only 75% of the training data, and it takes 2 days of training time (RDS) instead of 4 days (ABS).

I	A North Korean man **arrived in Seoul** Wednesday and **sought asylum** after escaping his hunger-stricken homeland, government officials said.
A	North Korean man **arrives in Seoul to seek asylum** for homeland security officials say.
D	North Korean man **defects to** South Korea.
I	**King Norodom Sihanouk** has **declined** requests to chair a summit of Cambodia 's top **political leaders**, saying the meeting would not bring any progress in deadlocked negotiations to form a government .
A	King Sihanouk **declines** to meet Cambodian leaders on eve of talks with Cambodia.
D	**Cambodian king refuses** to meet with leaders of **political leaders**.
I	Former U.S. president Jimmy Carter , who seems a perennial Nobel peace prize also-ran , **could have won** the coveted honor in 1978 **had it not been for strict deadline rules for nominations.**
A	Former U.S. president Jimmy Carter **wins** top honor for Nobel peace prize nominations.
D	Carter **wins** Nobel prize in literature.

Table 4: System generated article summaries. I: reference summary; A: RAS-Elman; and D: RDS.

For out-of-domain experiments, we compute ROUGE recall at 75 bytes and find that RDS performs poorly, even worse than the baseline method Prefix. This suggests that the decoupled architecture is sensitive to domain differences, and highlights a potential downside of the architecture. Investigating methods that can improve cross-domain performance is a direction for future work.

5 Discussion and Conclusion

We present some summaries for DUC documents generated by RAS-Elman and RDS in Table 4 to better understand possible reasons for the poor in-domain performance of RDS. The first observation is the shorter headlines generated by RDS compared to the DUC reference summaries and RAS-Elman headlines. RDS headlines are short — at an average length of 8.13 — and this is due to the short length of GIGAWORD titles it is trained on, at 8.50 words on average. On the other hand, the average length of DUC reference summaries and RAS-Elman headlines is 11.63 and 13.08 words respectively; this explains why RAS-Elman achieves better performance, since a longer sentence would have a better chance to score higher in ROUGE.

We also find that RDS often generates similar words and is penalised by ROUGE as it uses exact word matching, as is evidenced by *Sihanouk* and *Cambodian king* in the second example.[4] Lastly, the bag-of-words view of the `doc2vec` encoder results in some meaning loss: in the third example, *Jimmy Carter* did not actually win the Nobel peace prize, for example.

We also computed the source copy rate of the systems.[5] We find that, on average, RDS copies only 50.7% of its predicted words from input document, while ABS and ABS+ copy at a rate of 85.4% and 91.5%. This is interesting, as it suggests that it paraphrases more than other systems, while achieving similar ROUGE performance.

To summarise, we proposed decoupling the encoder–decoder architecture as is traditionally used in sequence-to-sequence problems. We tested the decoupled system on news title generation, and found that it performed competitively in-domain. Out-of-domain experiments, however, reveal sub-par performance, suggesting that the decoupled architecture is susceptible to domain differences.

References

Sumit Chopra, Michael Auli, and Alexander M. Rush. 2016. Abstractive sentence summarization with attentive recurrent neural networks. In *Proceedings of the 2016 Conference of the North American Chapter of the Association for Computational Linguistics: Human Language Technologies*, pages 93–98, San Diego, California, June. Association for Computational Linguistics.

Jeffrey Elman. 1998. Generalization, simple recurrent networks, and the emergence of structure. In *Proceedings of the Twentieth Annual Conference of the Cognitive Science Society*.

Cong Duy Vu Hoang, Trevor Cohn, and Gholamreza Haffari. 2016. Incorporating side information into recurrent neural network language models. In *Proceedings of the 2016 Conference of the North American Chapter of the Association for Computational Linguistics: Human Language Technologies*, pages 1250–1255, San Diego, California, June. Association for Computational Linguistics.

Sepp Hochreiter and Jürgen Schmidhuber. 1997. Long short-term memory. *Neural Computation*, 9:1735–1780.

[4]Informal manual evaluation for RDS, ABS, ABS+ and RAS on GIGAWORD reveals that ABS, ABS+ and RAS are also generating words that are of similar meaning, and that overall, RDS is less prefered by annotators.

[5]Source copy rate is defined as the fraction of generated words that are in the original source documents.

Jey Han Lau and Timothy Baldwin. 2016. An empirical evaluation of doc2vec with practical insights into document embedding generation. In *Proceedings of the 1st Workshop on Representation Learning for NLP*, pages 78–86, Berlin, Germany, August. Association for Computational Linguistics.

Quoc V Le and Tomas Mikolov. 2014. Distributed representations of sentences and documents. In *International Conference on Machine Learning*, pages 1188–1196.

Chin-Yew Lin. 2004. Rouge: A package for automatic evaluation of summaries. In Stan Szpakowicz Marie-Francine Moens, editor, *Text Summarization Branches Out: Proceedings of the ACL-04 Workshop*, pages 74–81, Barcelona, Spain, July. Association for Computational Linguistics.

Tomas Mikolov, Martin Karafiát, Lukas Burget, Jan Cernockỳ, and Sanjeev Khudanpur. 2010. Recurrent neural network based language model. In *Interspeech*, volume 2, page 3.

Tomas Mikolov, Ilya Sutskever, Kai Chen, Greg S Corrado, and Jeff Dean. 2013. Distributed representations of words and phrases and their compositionality. In *Advances in Neural Information Processing Systems*, pages 3111–3119.

Alexander M. Rush, Sumit Chopra, and Jason Weston. 2015. A neural attention model for abstractive sentence summarization. In *Proceedings of the 2015 Conference on Empirical Methods in Natural Language Processing*, pages 379–389, Lisbon, Portugal, September. Association for Computational Linguistics.

Omar F. Zaidan. 2009. Z-MERT: A fully configurable open source tool for minimum error rate training of machine translation systems. *The Prague Bulletin of Mathematical Linguistics*, 91:79–88.

Centroid-based Text Summarization through Compositionality of Word Embeddings

Gaetano Rossiello **Pierpaolo Basile** **Giovanni Semeraro**
Department of Computer Science
University of Bari, 70125 Bari, Italy
{firstname.secondname}@uniba.it

Abstract

The textual similarity is a crucial aspect for many extractive text summarization methods. A bag-of-words representation does not allow to grasp the semantic relationships between concepts when comparing strongly related sentences with no words in common. To overcome this issue, in this paper we propose a centroid-based method for text summarization that exploits the compositional capabilities of word embeddings. The evaluations on multi-document and multilingual datasets prove the effectiveness of the continuous vector representation of words compared to the bag-of-words model. Despite its simplicity, our method achieves good performance even in comparison to more complex deep learning models. Our method is unsupervised and it can be adopted in other summarization tasks.

1 Introduction

The goal of text summarization is to produce a shorter version of a source text by preserving the meaning and the key contents of the original text. This is a very complex problem since it requires to emulate the cognitive capacity of human beings to generate summaries. Thus, text summarization poses open challenges in both natural language understanding and generation. Due to the difficulty of this task, research work in the literature focused on the *extractive* aspect of summarization, where the generated summary is a selection of relevant sentences from a document (or a set of documents) in a copy-paste fashion. A good extractive summarization method must satisfy and optimize both coverage and diversity properties, where the selected sentences should cover a sufficient amount of topics from the original source text, avoiding the redundancy of information in the summary. The diversity property is fundamental especially for a multi-document summarization. For instance in a news aggregator, a selection of too similar sentences may compromise the quality of the generated summary.

An extractive method should define a sentence representation model, a technique for assigning a score to each sentence in the original source and a ranking module to properly select the most relevant sentences by relying on a similarity function. Following this vision, several summarization methods proposed in the literature use the bag of words (BOW) as representation model for the sentence scoring and selection modules (Radev et al., 2004; Erkan and Radev, 2004; Lin and Bilmes, 2011). Despite their proven effectiveness, these methods rely heavily on the notion of similarity between sentences, and a BOW representation is often not suitable to grasp the semantic relationships between concepts when comparing sentences. For example, taking into account the following two sentences *"Syd leaves Pink Floyd"* and *"Barrett abandons the band"*, in the BOW model their vector (sparse) representations result orthogonal since they have no words in common, nonetheless the two sentences are strongly related.

In attempt to solve this issue, in this work we propose a novel and simple extractive summarization method based on the geometric meaning of the centroid vector of a (multi) document by taking advantage of compositional properties of the word embeddings (Mikolov et al., 2013b). Empirically, we prove the effectiveness of word embeddings with a fair comparison to the BOW representation by limiting, as much as possible, the parameters and the complexity of the method. Surprisingly, the results achieved from our method on the gold standard DUC-2004 dataset are comparable,

Proceedings of the MultiLing 2017 Workshop on Summarization and Summary Evaluation Across Source Types and Genres, pages 12–21,
Valencia, Spain, April 3, 2017. ©2017 Association for Computational Linguistics

and in some cases better, to those obtained using a more complex sentence representations coming from the deep learning models.

In the following section we provide a brief description of word embeddings and text summarization methods. The centroid-based summarization method that uses word embeddings is described in Section 3, followed by experimental results in Section 4. Final remarks and a discussion about our future plans are reported in Section 5.

2 Related Work

2.1 Word Embeddings

Word embedding stands for a continuous vector representation able to capture syntactic and semantic information of a word. Several methods have been proposed in order to create word embeddings that follow the Distributional Hypothesis (Harris, 1954). In our work we use two models[1], continuous bag-of-words and skip-gram, introduced by (Mikolov et al., 2013a). These models learn a vector representation for each word using a neural network language model and can be trained efficiently on billions of words. Word2vec allows to learn complex semantic relationships using simple vectorial operators, such as vec(*king*) − vec(*man*) + vec(*woman*) ≈ vec(*queen*) and vec(*Barrett*) − vec(*singer*) + vec(*guitarist*) ≈ vec(*Gilmour*). However, our method is general and other approaches for building word embeddings can be used (Goldberg, 2015).

2.2 Text Summarization

Since the first method proposed by (Luhn, 1958), automatic text summarization has been widely addressed by the research community with the proposal of different methodologies as well as toolkits (Saggion and Gaizauskas, 2004). Good surveys are proposed by (Jones, 2007; Saggion and Poibeau, 2013). Since our method exploits word embeddings as alternative representation to BOW, here we focus on the methods sharing this feature. Methods based on matrix factorization, such as Latent Semantic Analysis (LSA) (Ozsoy et al., 2011) and Non-Negative Matrix Factorization (NMF) (Lee et al., 2009), have the aim to arise the latent factors by producing dense and compact representations of sentences. Recently, riding the wave of prominent results of modern Deep Learning (DL) models in many natural language processing tasks (LeCun et al., 2015; Goodfellow et al., 2016), several groups have started to exploit deep neural networks for both *abstractive* (Rush et al., 2015; Nallapati et al., 2016) and *extractive* (Kågebäck et al., 2014; Cao et al., 2015; Cheng and Lapata, 2016) text summarization.

[1]Commonly called *word2vec*.

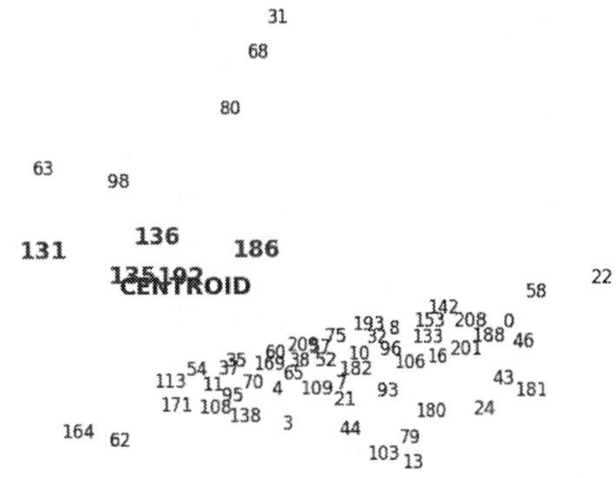

Figure 1: Sentence and centroid embeddings 2D visualization of the *Donkey Kong (video game)* Wikipedia article. Dimensionality reduction is performed using t-SNE algorithm. For each sentence the position in the document is shown. The closest sentences to centroid embedding are marked in green.

3 Centroid-based Method

The centroid-based method for extractive summarization was introduced by (Radev et al., 2004). The centroid represents a pseudo-document which condenses the meaningful information of a document[2]. The main idea is to project in the vector space the vector representations of both the centroid and each sentence of a document. Then, the sentences closer to the centroid are selected. The original method adopts the BOW model for the vector representations using the $tf * idf$ weight scheme (Salton and McGill, 1986), where the size of vectors is equal to that of the document vocabulary. We adapt the centroid-based method introducing a distributed representation of words where each word in a document is represented by a vector of real numbers of an established size. Formally, given a corpus of documents $[D_1, D_2, \dots]$ and its vocabulary V with size $N = |V|$, we define a matrix $E \in \mathbb{R}^{N,k}$, so-called *lookup table*, where the i-th row is a word embedding of size k, $k << N$,

[2]In this section we refer to a single document, but the method can be extended to a cluster of documents.

arcade	donkey	kong	game	nintendo	coleco	*centroid embedding*
arcades	goat	hong	gameplay	mario	intellivision	nes
pac-man	pig	macao	multiplayer	wii	atari	gamecube
console	monkey	fung	videogame	console	nes	konami
famicom	horse	taiwan	rpg	nes	msx	wii
sega	cow	wong	gamespot	gamecube	3do	famicom

Table 1: Centroid words of the *Donkey Kong (video game)* article having the tf-idf values greater than a topic threshold equal to 0.3. For each centroid word, the five closest words are shown using the skip-gram model trained on the Wikipedia (en) content. In the last column the words most similar to the centroid embedding computed using element-wise addition are shown.

of the i-th word in V. The values of the word embeddings matrix E are learned using the neural network model introduced by (Mikolov et al., 2013b). The model can be trained on the collection of documents to be summarized or on a larger corpus. This is a peculiar advantage of Representation Learning (RL) (Bengio et al., 2013) that allows to reuse an external knowledge and this is especially useful for the summarization of documents in specific domains, where large amount of data are not available. After learning the lookup table, our summarization method consists of four steps: 1) preprocess the input document; 2) build the centroid embedding; 3) compute the sentence scores; 4) select the relevant sentences.

3.1 Preprocessing

The first step follows the common pipeline for the summarization task: split the document into sentences, convert all words in lower case and remove stopwords. Stemming is not performed because we let the word embeddings to discover the linguistic regularities of words with the same root (Mikolov et al., 2013c). For instance, the most similar embeddings to the words that compose the centroid vector using the skip-gram model trained on the Wikipedia content are reported in Table 1. The closest word of *arcade* is its plural *arcades*, while they are orthogonal in the vector space according to the BOW representation.

3.2 Centroid Embedding

In order to build a centroid vector using word embeddings, we first select the meaningful words into the document. For simplicity and a fair comparison with the original method, we select those words having the $tf * idf$ weight greater than a topic threshold. Thus, we compute the centroid embedding as the sum[3] of the embeddings of the top ranked words in the document using the lookup table E.

$$C = \sum_{w \in D, tfidf(w) > t} E[idx(w)] \quad (1)$$

In the eq. (1) we denote with C the centroid embedding related to the document D and with $idx(w)$ a function that returns the index of the word w in the vocabulary. In the headers of the Table 1 the centroid words extracted from a Wikipedia article are reported. The last column shows the words most similar to centroid embedding computed using element-wise addition. It is important to underline that all five closest words to the centroid vector are semantically related to the main topic of the document despite the size of the Wikipedia vocabulary (about 1 million words).

3.3 Sentence Scoring

For each sentence in the document, we create an embedding representation by summing the vectors for each word in the sentence stored in the lookup table E.

$$S_j = \sum_{w \in S_j} E[idx(w)] \quad (2)$$

In the eq. (2) we denote with S_j the j-th sentence in the document D. Then, the sentence score is computed as the cosine similarity between the embedding of the sentence S_j and that of the centroid C of the document D.

$$sim(C, S_j) = \frac{C^T \bullet S_j}{||C|| \cdot ||S_j||} \quad (3)$$

Figure 1 shows a visualization of sentence and centroid embeddings of a Wikipedia article. We

[3]Some works use the average rather than the addition to compose word embeddings. However, the sum and the average do not change the similarity value when using the cosine distance, since the angle between vectors remains the same.

Sent ID	Sentence	Score
136	The original **arcade** version of the **game** appears in the **Nintendo** 64 **game Donkey Kong** 64.	0.9533
131	The **game** was ported to **Nintendo**'s Family Computer (*Famicom*) *console* in 1983 as one of the system's three launch titles; the same version was a launch title for the *Famicom*'s North American version, the **Nintendo** Entertainment System (*NES*).	0.9375
186	In 2004, **Nintendo** released *Mario* vs. **Donkey Kong**, a sequel to the **Game** Boy title.	0.9366
192	In 2007, **Donkey Kong** Barrel Blast was released for the **Nintendo** *Wii*.	0.9362
135	The *NES* version was re-released as an unlockable game in Animal Crossing for the *GameCube* and as an item for purchase on the *Wii*'s Virtual *Console*.	0.9308

Table 2: The most relevant sentences of the *Donkey Kong* article selected with the centroid-based summarization method using word embeddings. For each sentence are reported the related position ID in the document and the similarity score computed between sentence and centroid embeddings. The words that compose the centroid vector are marked in **bold**. The most similar words to the centroid ones are reported in *italic*.

use t-SNE method (van der Maaten and Hinton, 2008) to reduce the dimensionality of vectors from 300 to 2. For each sentence the position ID in the document is shown. The closest sentences to the centroid embedding are marked in green. The words that compose the centroid are the same showed in Table 1. In Table 2 we report the sentences near to the centroid with the related cosine similarity values. As we expected, the most relevant sentence (136) contains many words close to the centroid vector. However, the relevant aspect concerns the last sentence (135). Despite this sentence does not contain any centroid word, it has a high similarity value so it is close to the centroid embedding in the vector space. The reason is due to the presence of the words, such as *NES*, *GameCube* and *Wii*, that are the closest words to the centroid embedding (Table 1). This proves the effectiveness of the compositionality of word embeddings to encode the semantic relations between words through vector dense representations.

3.4 Sentence Selection

The sentences are sorted in descending order of their similarity scores. The top ranked sentences are iteratively selected and added to the summary until the limit[4] is reached. In order to satisfy the redundancy property, during the iteration we compute the cosine similarity between the next sentence and each one already in the summary. We discard the incoming sentence if the similarity value is greater than a threshold. This procedure is reported in Algorithm 1. However, similar sentence selection approaches are described in (Carbonell and Goldstein, 1998; Saggion and Gaizauskas, 2004).

Algorithm 1 Sentence selection

```
Input: S, Scores, st, limit
Output: Summary
  S ← SORTDESC(S,Scores)
  k ← 1
  for i ← 1 to m do
      length ← LENGTH(Summary)
      if length > limit then return Summary
      SV ← SUMVECTORS(S[i])
      include ← True
      for j ← 1 to k do
          SV2 ← SUMVECTORS(Summary[j])
          sim ← SIMILARITY(SV,SV2)
          if sim > st then
              include ← False
      if include then
          Summary[k] ← S[i]
          k ← k + 1
```

4 Experiments

In this section we describe the benchmarks conducted on two text summarization tasks. The main goal is to compare the centroid-based method using two different representations (bag-of-words and word embeddings). In Section 4.1 and in Section 4.2 we report the experimental results carried out on Multi-Document and Multilingual Single Document summarization tasks, respectively.

[4]The limit can be the number of bytes/words in the summary or a compression rate.

4.1 Multi-Document Summarization

Dataset and Metrics During the document understanding conference (DUC)[5] from 2001 to 2007, several gold standard datasets have been developed to evaluate the summarization methods. In particular, we evaluate our method on multi-document summarization using the DUC-2004 Task 2 dataset composed by 50 clusters, each of which consists of 10 documents coming from Associated Press and New York Times newswires. For each cluster, four summaries written by different humans were supplied. For the evaluation, we adopt the ROUGE (Lin, 2004), a set of recall-based metrics that compare the automatic and human summaries on the basis of the n-gram overlap. In our experiment, we adopt both ROUGE-1 and ROUGE-2[6].

Baselines For the comparison, we propose several baselines. Firstly, we adapt the centroid method proposed by (Radev et al., 2004) (**C_BOW**) for a fair comparison. In the original work, the sentence scores are the linear combination of the centroid score, the positional value and the first sentence overlap. The centroid score is the sum of $tf * idf$ weights of the words occurring both in the sentence and in the centroid. In our experiment, we apply both our sentence score and selection algorithms. **LEAD** simply chooses the first 665 bytes from the most recent article in each cluster. **SumBasic** is a simple probabilistic method proposed by (Nenkova and Vanderwende, 2005) commonly used as baseline in the summarization evaluation. **Peer65** is the winning system in DUC-2004 Task 2. To compare our method with others which also use compact and dense representations, we use the method proposed by (Lee et al., 2009) that adopts the generic relevance of sentences method using **NMF**. Another method often used in summarization evaluations is **LexRank** proposed by (Erkan and Radev, 2004) which uses the TextRank algorithm (Mihalcea and Tarau, 2004) to establish a ranking between sentences. Finally, we compare our method with the one proposed by (Cao et al., 2015) that uses Recursive Neural Network (**RNN**) for learning sentence embeddings by encoding syntactic features.

[5]http://duc.nist.gov

[6]ROUGE-1.5.5 with options -c 95 -b 665 -m -n 2 -x

System	R1	R2	tt	st	size
LEAD	32.42	6.42			
SumBasic	37.27	8.58			
Peer65	38.22	9.18			
NMF	31.60	6.31			
LexRank	37.58	8.78			
RNN	38.78	9.86			
C_BOW	37.76	8.08	0.1	0.6	
C_GNEWS	37.91	8.45	0.2	0.9	300
C_CBOW	38.68	8.93	0.3	0.93	200
C_SKIP	**38.81**	**9.97**	0.3	0.94	400

Table 3: ROUGE scores (%) on DUC-2004 dataset. **tt** and **st** are the topic and similarity thresholds respectively. **size** is the dimension of embeddings.

Implementation Our system[7] is written in Python by relying on *nltk*, *scikit-learn* and *gensim* libraries for text preprocessing, building the sentence-term matrix and import the word2vec model. We train the word embeddings on DUC-2004 corpus using the original word2vec[8] implementation. We test both continuous bag-of-words (**C_CBOW**) and skip-gram (**C_SKIP**) neural architectures proposed in (Mikolov et al., 2013a) using the same parameters[9] but varying the embedding sizes. Moreover, we compare our method using the model trained on a part of Google News dataset (**C_GNEWS**) which consists of about 100 billion words. In the preprocessing step each cluster of documents is divided in sentences and stopwords are removed. We do not perform stemming as reported in Section 3. To find the best parameters configuration, we run a grid search using this setting: embedding size in [100, 200, 300, 400, 500], topic and similarity thresholds respectively in [0, 0.5] and [0.5, 1] with a step of 0.01.

Results and Discussion The results of the experiment are shown in Table 3. We report the best scores of our method using the three different word2vec models along with their parameters. For all word embeddings models, our method outperforms the original centroid one. In detail, with the skip-gram model we obtain an increment of 1.05% and 1.71% with respect to the BOW model using ROUGE-1 and ROUGE-2 respectively. Moreover, our simple method with skip-gram performs bet-

[7]https://github.com/gaetangate/text-summarizer

[8]https://code.google.com/archive/p/word2vec/

[9]-hs 1 -min-count 0 -window 10 -negative 10 -iter 10

ter than the more complex models based on RNN. This proves the effectiveness of the compositional capability of word embeddings in order to encode the information word sequences by applying a simple sum of word vectors, as already proved in (Wieting et al., 2015). Although our method with the model pre-trained on Google News does not achieve the best score, it is interesting to notice the flexibility of the word embeddings in reusing external knowledge. Regarding the comparison between BOW and embedding representations, the experiment shows different behaviors of the similarity threshold. In particular, the use of word2vec requires a higher threshold because the word embeddings are dense vectors unlike the sparse representation of BOW. This proves that the embeddings of sentences are closer in the vector space, thus the cosine similarity returns closer values.

System	R1	R2	tt	st	size
C_BOW	37.56	**8.26**	0	0.6	
C_GNEWS	36.91	7.35	0	0.9	300
C_CBOW	**37.69**	7.64	0	0.83	300
C_SKIP	37.61	8.10	0	0.91	300

Table 4: ROUGE scores without topic threshold.

Also the topic threshold shows different trends. The word embeddings require a higher threshold value to make our method effective. In order to analyze this aspect we run another experiment setting the topic threshold to 0. The results are reported in Table 4. Results show that the BOW representation is more stable and obtains the best ROUGE-2 score, while the performance obtained by word2vec decreases considerably. This means that word embeddings are more sensitive to noise and they require an accurate choice of the meaningful words to compose the centroid vector.

Summaries Overlap Although the different methods achieve similar ROUGE scores, they not necessarily generate similar summaries. An example is reported in Table 6. In this section we conduct a further analysis by comparing the summaries generated by the best four configurations of the centroid method reported in Table 3. We adopt the same criterion presented in (Hong et al., 2014), where the different summaries are compared in terms of sentences and words overlap using the Jaccard coefficient. Due to space constraint, we report in Table 5 only the sentence overlap. The results prove that different word representations lead to different summaries. In particular, the summaries using BOW differ considerably from those generated using word2vec, but this is true even for different embedding models. On the other hand, only the models trained on the DUC-2004 corpus (CBOW and SKIP) tend to generate more similar summaries. This analysis suggests that a combination of various models trained on different corpora could result in good performance.

	GNEWS	CBOW	SKIP	BOW
GNEWS	1	0.109	0.171	0.075
CBOW		1	0.460	0.072
SKIP			1	0.105
BOW				1

Table 5: Sentence overlap.

4.2 Multilingual Document Summarization

Task Description We carried out an experiment on Multilingual Single-document Summarization (MSS). Our main goal is to prove empirically the effectiveness of the use of word embeddings in the document summarization task across different languages. For this purpose, we evaluate our method on the MSS task proposed in MultiLing 2015 (Giannakopoulos et al., 2015), a special session at SIGDIAL 2015. Starting from 2011 the aim of MultiLing community is to promote the cutting-edge research in automatic summarization by providing datasets and by introducing several pilot tasks to encourage further developments in single and multi-document summarization and in summarizing human dialogs in on-line forums and customer call centers. The goal of the MSS 2015 task is to generate a single document summary from a selection of some of the best written Wikipedia articles with at least one out of 38 languages defined by organizers of the task. The dataset[10] is divided into a training and a test sets, both consisting of 30 documents for each of 38 languages. For both datasets, the body of the articles and the related abstracts with the character length limits are provided. Since the Wikipedia abstracts are summaries written by humans, they are useful to perform automatic evaluations. We evaluate our method using five different languages: English, Italian, German, Spanish and French.

[10]http://multiling.iit.demokritos.gr/pages/view/1532/task-mss-single-document-summarization-data-and-information

BOW - Bag of Words baseline
The controversy centers on the payment of nearly dlrs 400,000 in scholarships to relatives of IOC members by the Salt Lake bid committee which won the right to stage the 2002 games. Pound said the panel would investigate allegations that "there may or may not have been payments for the benefit of members of the IOC or their families connected with the Salt Lake City bid." Samaranch said he was surprised at the allegations of corruption in the International Olympic Committee made by senior Swiss member Marc Hodler.
CBOW - Continuous Bag of Words trained on DUC-2004 dataset
Marc Hodler, a senior member of the International Olympic Committee executive board, alleged malpractices in the voting for the 1996 Atlanta Games, 2000 Sydney Olympics and 2002 Salt Lake Games. The IOC, meanwhile, said it was prepared to investigate allegations made by Hodler of bribery in the selection of Olympic host cities. The issue of vote-buying came to the fore in Lausanne because of the recent disclosure of scholarship payments made to six relatives of IOC members by Salt Lake City officials during their successful bid to play host to the 2002 Winter Games.
SKIP - Skip-gram trained on DUC-2004 dataset
Marc Hodler, a senior member of the International Olympic Committee executive board, alleged malpractices in the voting for the 1996 Atlanta Games, 2000 Sydney Olympics and 2002 Salt Lake Games. The IOC, meanwhile, said it was prepared to investigate allegations made by Hodler of bribery in the selection of Olympic host cities. Saying "if we have to clean, we will clean," Juan Antonio Samaranch responded on Sunday to allegations of corruption in the Olympic bidding process by declaring that IOC members who were found to have accepted bribes from candidate cities could be expelled.
GNEWS - Skip-gram trained on Google News dataset
The International Olympic Committee has ordered a top-level investigation into the payment of nearly dlrs 400,000 in scholarships to relatives of IOC members by the Salt Lake group which won the bid for the 2002 Winter Games. The mayor of the Japanese city of Nagano, site of the 1998 Winter Olympics, denied allegations that city officials bribed members of the International Olympic Committee to win the right to host the games. Swiss IOC executive board member Marc Hodler said Sunday he might be thrown out of the International Olympic Committee for making allegations of corruption within the Olympic movement.

Table 6: Summaries of the cluster **d30038** in DUC-2004 dataset using the centroid-based summarization method with different sentence representations.

Model Configuration In order to learn word embeddings for the different languages, we exploit five Wikipedia dumps[11], one for each chosen language. We extract the plain text from the Wiki markup language using Wikiextractor[12], a Wikimedia parser written in Python. Each article is converted from UTF-8 to ASCII encoding using the Unidecode Python package. Since in the previous evaluation we observe a similar behavior between the continuous bag of words and skip-gram models, in this evaluation we adopt only the skip-gram one using the same training parameters[13] for all five languages. The Table 7 reports the Wikipedia statistics for the five languages regarding the number of words and the size of the vocabularies.

Language	# Words	Vocabulary
English	1,890,356,976	973,839
Italian	371,218,773	378,286
German	657,234,125	1,042,683
Spanish	464,465,399	419,683
French	551,057,299	458,748

Table 7: Wikipedia statistics.

Experiment Protocol In order to reproduce the same challenging scenario of the MultiLing 2015 MSS task, we performed the tuning of parameters using only the training set. To find the best topic and similarity threshold parameters we run a grid search as explained in Section 4.1. The grid search is performed for each language separately using both BOW and skip-gram representations. The parameter configurations are in line with those of the previous experiment on DUC-2004. In detail, the topic thresholds are in the range [0.1, 0.2] using the BOW model and in the range [0.3, 0.5] using word embeddings. While, the similarity thresholds are slightly higher w.r.t. the multi-document experiment: about 0.7 and 0.95 for BOW and skip-gram, respectively. This is due to the fact that too similar sentences are rare, especially with well-written documents as Wikipedia articles. The best parameters configuration for each language is used to generate summaries for the documents in the test set. Also for this task, each document is preprocessed with the sentences segmentation and stopwords removal, without stemming. We adopt the same automatic evaluation metrics used by the participating systems in MSS 2015 task: ROUGE-1, -2, -SU4[14]. ROUGE-SU4 computes the score between the generated and human summaries considering the overlap of the skip-bigrams of 4 as well as the unigrams. Finally, the generated summary for each document must comply with a specific length constraint (rather than using a unique length limit for the whole collection). This differs

[11] https://dumps.wikimedia.org/_lang_wiki/20161220/ with _lang_ in [en, it, de, es, fr]

[12] https://github.com/attardi/wikiextractor/wiki

[13] -hs 1 -min-count 10 -window 8 -negative 5 -iter 5

[14] ROUGE-1.5.7 with options -n 2 -2 4 -u -x -m

	English		Italian		German		Spanish		French	
	R1	R2	R1	R2	R1	R2	R1	R2	R1	R2
LEAD	44.33	11.68	30.46	4.38	29.13	3.21	43.02	9.17	42.73	8.07
WORST	37.17	9.93	39.68	10.01	33.02	4.88	45.20	13.04	46.68	12.96
BEST	50.38	15.10	43.87	12.50	40.58	8.80	53.23	17.86	51.39	15.38
C_BOW	49.06	13.43	33.44	4.82	35.28	4.93	48.38	12.88	46.13	10.45
C_W2V	**50.43**‡	13.34†	**35.12**	**6.81**	**35.38**†	**5.39**†	**49.25**†	**12.99**	**47.82**†	**12.15**
ORACLE	61.91	22.42	53.31	17.51	54.34	13.32	62.55	22.36	58.68	17.18

Table 8: ROUGE-1, -2 scores (%) on MultiLing MSS 2015 dataset for five different languages.

from the previous evaluation on DUC-2004.

Results and Discussion The results for each languages are shown in Table 8. We report the ROUGE-1, -2 scores for each chosen language. **LEAD** and **C_BOW** represent the same baselines used in the multi-document experiment. The former uses the initial text of each article truncated to the length of the Wikipedia abstract. The latter is the centroid-based method with the BOW representation. Our method that uses word embeddings learned with skip-gram model is labeled with **C_W2V**. For each metric and language we also report the **WORST** and the **BEST** scores[15] obtained by the 23 participating systems at MSS 2015 task. Finally, **ORACLE** scores can be considered as an upper bound approximation for the extractive summarization methods. It uses a covering algorithm (Davis et al., 2012) that selects sentences from the original text covering the words in the summary without disregarding the length limit. We highlight in bold the scores of our method when it outperforms the baseline **C_BOW**. On the other hand, the superscripts † and ‡ imply a better performance of our method with respect to the **WORST** and the **BEST** scores respectively.

Both centroid-based methods overcome the simple baseline over all languages. Our method always achieves better scores against the BOW model except for ROUGE-2 metric for English. This confirms the effectiveness of using word embeddings as alternative sentence representations able to capture the semantic similarities between the centroid words and the sentences, when summarizing single documents too. Moreover, our method outperforms substantially the lowest scores performing systems participating in MSS 2015 task for English and German languages. For English our method obtains a ROUGE-1 score even better than the one of the best system in MSS 2015. Instead, our method fails in summarizing Italian documents and it achieves the worst ROUGE-2 for Spanish and French languages. The reason may lie in the size of the Wikipedia dumps used to learn the word embeddings for different languages. As showing in Table 7, the sizes of the various corpora as well as the ratios between the number of words and dimension of the vocabularies, differ consistently. The English version of Wikipedia consists of nearly 2 billion words against about 300 million words of Italian one. Thus, according to the distributional hypothesis reported in (Harris, 1954), we expect better performance for our method in summarizing English or German articles with respect to the other languages where the word embeddings are learned using a smaller corpus. Our results and in particular the ROUGE-SU4 scores reported in Figure 2 support this hypothesis.

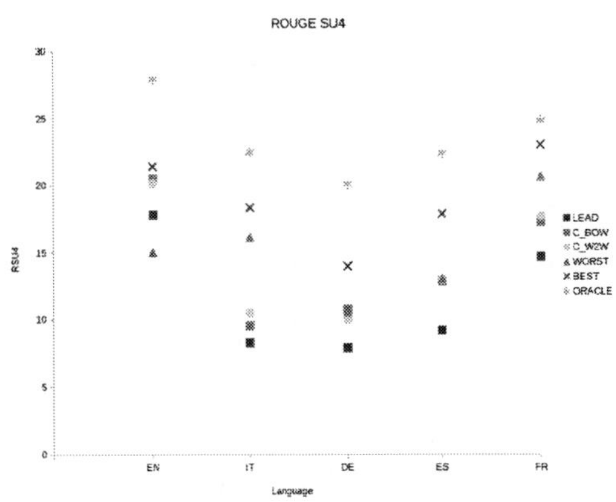

Figure 2: ROUGE-SU4 scores (%) comparison on MultiLing MSS 2015 dataset.

[15]http://multiling.iit.demokritos.gr/file/view/1629/mss-multilingual-single-document-summarization-submission-and-automatic-score

5 Conclusion

In this paper, we propose a centroid-based method for extractive summarization which exploits the compositional capability of word embeddings. One of the advantages of our method lies on its simplicity. Indeed, it can be used as a baseline in experimenting new articulate semantic representations in summarization tasks. Moreover, following the idea of representation learning, it is feasible to infuse knowledge by training the word embeddings from external sources. Finally, the proposed method is fully unsupervised, thus it can be adopted in other summarization tasks, such as query-based document summarization. As future work, we plan to evaluate the centroid-based summarization method using a topic model, such as Latent Dirichlet Allocation (LDA) (Blei et al., 2003) or Non-negative Matrix Factorization (NMF) (Berry et al., 2007), in order to extract the meaningful words to compute the centroid embedding as well as to carry out a comprehensive comparison of different sentence representations using more complex neural language models (Le and Mikolov, 2014; Zhang and LeCun, 2015; Józefowicz et al., 2016). Finally, the combination of distributional and relational semantics (Fried and Duh, 2014; Verga and McCallum, 2016; Rossiello, 2016) applied to extractive text summarization is a promising further direction that we want to investigate.

References

Y. Bengio, A. Courville, and P. Vincent. 2013. Representation learning: A review and new perspectives. *IEEE Transactions on Pattern Analysis and Machine Intelligence*, 35(8):1798–1828, Aug.

Michael W. Berry, Murray Browne, Amy N. Langville, V. Paul Pauca, and Robert J. Plemmons. 2007. Algorithms and applications for approximate nonnegative matrix factorization. *Computational Statistics & Data Analysis*, 52(1):155–173, September.

David M. Blei, Andrew Y. Ng, and Michael I. Jordan. 2003. Latent dirichlet allocation. *J. Mach. Learn. Res.*, 3:993–1022, March.

Ziqiang Cao, Furu Wei, Li Dong, Sujian Li, and Ming Zhou. 2015. Ranking with recursive neural networks and its application to multi-document summarization. In *Proceedings of the Twenty-Ninth AAAI Conference on Artificial Intelligence*, AAAI'15, pages 2153–2159. AAAI Press.

Jaime Carbonell and Jade Goldstein. 1998. The use of mmr, diversity-based reranking for reordering documents and producing summaries. In *Proceedings of the 21st Annual International ACM SIGIR Conference on Research and Development in Information Retrieval*, SIGIR '98, pages 335–336, New York, NY, USA. ACM.

Jianpeng Cheng and Mirella Lapata. 2016. Neural summarization by extracting sentences and words. pages 484–494, August.

S. T. Davis, J. M. Conroy, and J. D. Schlesinger. 2012. Occams – an optimal combinatorial covering algorithm for multi-document summarization. In *2012 IEEE 12th International Conference on Data Mining Workshops*, pages 454–463, Dec.

Gunes Erkan and Dragomir R. Radev. 2004. Lexrank: Graph-based lexical centrality as salience in text summarization. *J. Artif. Int. Res.*, 22(1):457–479, December.

Daniel Fried and Kevin Duh. 2014. Incorporating both distributional and relational semantics in word representations. *CoRR*, abs/1412.4369.

George Giannakopoulos, Jeff Kubina, John M. Conroy, Josef Steinberger, Benoît Favre, Mijail A. Kabadjov, Udo Kruschwitz, and Massimo Poesio. 2015. Multiling 2015: Multilingual summarization of single and multi-documents, on-line fora, and call-center conversations. In *Proceedings of the SIGDIAL 2015 Conference.*, pages 270–274.

Yoav Goldberg. 2015. A primer on neural network models for natural language processing. *CoRR*, abs/1510.00726.

Ian Goodfellow, Yoshua Bengio, and Aaron Courville. 2016. *Deep Learning*. MIT Press. `http://www.deeplearningbook.org`.

Zellig Harris. 1954. Distributional structure. *Word*, 10(23):146–162.

Kai Hong, John Conroy, Benoit Favre, Alex Kulesza, Hui Lin, and Ani Nenkova. 2014. A repository of state of the art and competitive baseline summaries for generic news summarization. In Nicoletta Calzolari (Conference Chair), Khalid Choukri, Thierry Declerck, Hrafn Loftsson, Bente Maegaard, Joseph Mariani, Asuncion Moreno, Jan Odijk, and Stelios Piperidis, editors, *Proceedings of the Ninth International Conference on Language Resources and Evaluation (LREC'14)*, Reykjavik, Iceland, may. European Language Resources Association (ELRA).

Karen Spärck Jones. 2007. Automatic summarising: The state of the art. *Information Processing & Management*, 43(6):1449–1481.

Rafal Józefowicz, Oriol Vinyals, Mike Schuster, Noam Shazeer, and Yonghui Wu. 2016. Exploring the limits of language modeling. *CoRR*, abs/1602.02410.

Mikael Kågebäck, Olof Mogren, Nina Tahmasebi, and Devdatt Dubhashi. 2014. Extractive summarization using continuous vector space models. In *Proceedings of the 2nd Workshop on Continuous Vector Space Models and their Compositionality (CVSC)@ EACL*, pages 31–39.

Quoc Le and Tomas Mikolov. 2014. Distributed representations of sentences and documents. In Tony Jebara and Eric P. Xing, editors, *Proceedings of the 31st International Conference on Machine Learning (ICML-14)*, pages 1188–1196. JMLR Workshop and Conference Proceedings.

Yann LeCun, Yoshua Bengio, and Geoffrey Hinton. 2015. Deep learning. *Nature*, 521:436–444.

Ju-Hong Lee, Sun Park, Chan-Min Ahn, and Daeho Kim. 2009. Automatic generic document summarization based on non-negative matrix factorization. *Inf. Process. Manage.*, 45(1):20–34, January.

Hui Lin and Jeff Bilmes. 2011. A class of submodular functions for document summarization. In *Proceedings of the 49th Annual Meeting of the Association for Computational Linguistics: Human Language Technologies*, pages 510–520, Portland, Oregon, USA, June. Association for Computational Linguistics.

Chin-Yew Lin. 2004. Rouge: A package for automatic evaluation of summaries. In Stan Szpakowicz Marie-Francine Moens, editor, *Text Summarization Branches Out: Proceedings of the ACL-04 Workshop*, pages 74–81, Barcelona, Spain, July. Association for Computational Linguistics.

H. P. Luhn. 1958. The automatic creation of literature abstracts. *IBM J. Res. Dev.*, 2(2):159–165, April.

Rada Mihalcea and Paul Tarau. 2004. Textrank: Bringing order into texts. In Dekang Lin and Dekai Wu, editors, *Proceedings of EMNLP 2004*, pages 404–411, Barcelona, Spain, July. Association for Computational Linguistics.

Tomas Mikolov, Kai Chen, Greg Corrado, and Jeffrey Dean. 2013a. Efficient estimation of word representations in vector space. *arXiv preprint arXiv:1301.3781*.

Tomas Mikolov, Ilya Sutskever, Kai Chen, Greg S Corrado, and Jeff Dean. 2013b. Distributed representations of words and phrases and their compositionality. In *Advances in neural information processing systems*, pages 3111–3119.

Tomas Mikolov, Wen-tau Yih, and Geoffrey Zweig. 2013c. Linguistic regularities in continuous space word representations. In *Proceedings of the 2013 Conference of the North American Chapter of the Association for Computational Linguistics: Human Language Technologies*, pages 746–751, Atlanta, Georgia, June. Association for Computational Linguistics.

Ramesh Nallapati, Bowen Zhou, Cicero dos Santos, Caglar Gulcehre, and Bing Xiang. 2016. Abstractive text summarization using sequence-to-sequence rnns and beyond. pages 280–290, August.

Ani Nenkova and Lucy Vanderwende. 2005. The impact of frequency on summarization. *Microsoft Research, Redmond, Washington, Tech. Rep. MSR-TR-2005-101*.

Makbule G. Ozsoy, Ferda N. Alpaslan, and Ilyas Cicekli. 2011. Text summarization using latent semantic analysis. *Journal of Information Science*, 37(4):405–417.

Dragomir R. Radev, Hongyan Jing, Malgorzata Stys, and Daniel Tam. 2004. Centroid-based summarization of multiple documents. *Inf. Process. Manage.*, 40(6):919–938, November.

Gaetano Rossiello. 2016. Neural abstractive text summarization. In *Proceedings of the Doctoral Consortium of AI*IA 2016 co-located with the 15th International Conference of the Italian Association for Artificial Intelligence (AI*IA 2016), Genova, Italy, November 29, 2016.*, pages 70–75.

Alexander M. Rush, Sumit Chopra, and Jason Weston. 2015. A neural attention model for abstractive sentence summarization. In *Proceedings of the 2015 Conference on Empirical Methods in Natural Language Processing*, pages 379–389, Lisbon, Portugal, September. Association for Computational Linguistics.

Horacio Saggion and Robert Gaizauskas. 2004. Multidocument summarization by cluster/profile relevance and redundancy removal. In *Proceedings of the HLT/NAACL Document Understanding Workshop (DUC 2004)*, Boston, May.

Horacio Saggion and Thierry Poibeau. 2013. Automatic text summarization: Past, present and future. In *Multi-source, Multilingual Information Extraction and Summarization*, pages 3–21. Springer.

Gerard Salton and Michael J. McGill. 1986. *Introduction to Modern Information Retrieval*. McGraw-Hill, Inc., New York, NY, USA.

Laurens van der Maaten and Geoffrey E. Hinton. 2008. Visualizing high-dimensional data using t-sne. *Journal of Machine Learning Research*, 9:2579–2605.

Patrick Verga and Andrew McCallum. 2016. Row-less universal schema. *CoRR*, abs/1604.06361.

John Wieting, Mohit Bansal, Kevin Gimpel, and Karen Livescu. 2015. Towards universal paraphrastic sentence embeddings. *CoRR*, abs/1511.08198.

Xiang Zhang and Yann LeCun. 2015. Text understanding from scratch. *CoRR*, abs/1502.01710.

Query-based summarization using MDL principle

Natalia Vanetik
Shamoon College of Engineering
Beer Sheva
Israel
natalyav@sce.ac.il

Marina Litvak
Shamoon College of Engineering
Beer Sheva
Israel
marinal@sce.ac.il

Abstract

Query-based text summarization is aimed at extracting essential information that answers the query from original text. The answer is presented in a minimal, often predefined, number of words. In this paper we introduce a new unsupervised approach for query-based extractive summarization, based on the minimum description length (MDL) principle that employs Krimp compression algorithm (Vreeken et al., 2011). The key idea of our approach is to select frequent word sets related to a given query that compress document sentences better and therefore describe the document better. A summary is extracted by selecting sentences that best cover query-related frequent word sets. The approach is evaluated based on the DUC 2005 and DUC 2006 datasets which are specifically designed for query-based summarization (DUC, 2005 2006). It competes with the best results.

1 Introduction

Query-based summarization (QS) is directed toward generating a summary most relevant to a given query. It can relate to a single-document or to a multi-document input. Our approach for QS is based on the MDL principle, defining the best summary as the one that leads to the *best compression* of the text *with query-related information* by providing its *shortest and most concise description*. The MDL principle is widely useful in compression techniques of non-textual data, such as summarization of query results for online analytical processing (OLAP) applications (Lakshmanan et al., 2002; Bu et al., 2005). However, only a few works about text summarization using MDL can be found in the literature. Nomoto and Matsumoto (2001) used K-means clustering extended with the MDL principle, to find diverse topics in the summarized text. Nomoto (2004) also extended the C4.5 classifier with MDL for learning rhetorical relations. In (Nguyen et al., 2015) the problem of micro-review summarization is formulated within the MDL framework, where the authors view the tips as being encoded by snippets, and seek to find a collection of snippets that produces the encoding with the minimum number of bits.

This work proposes a MDL approach where the sentences that are best described by the query-related word sequences are selected to a summary. It is principally different from the mentioned works by (1) using frequent itemsets and not single words in the description model, (2) compressing entire documents instead of summaries, (3) ranking method for sentences, and (4) the description model itself. We tested our approach on DUC 2005 and DUC 2006 data for English query-based summarization.

2 Related Work

Multiple works about QS have been published in recent years. Daumé III and Marcu (2006) presented BayeSum, a model for sentence extraction in QS. BayeSum is based on the concepts of three models: language model, Bayesian statistical model, and graphical model. Mohamed and Rajasekaran (2006) proposed an approach for QS based on document graphs, which are directed graphs of concepts or entity nodes and relations between them. The work in (Bosma, 2005) introduced a graph search algorithm that looks for relevant sentences in the discourse structure represented as a graph. The author used Rhetorical Structure Theory for creating a graph representation of a text document - a weighted graph with

Proceedings of the MultiLing 2017 Workshop on Summarization and Summary Evaluation Across Source Types and Genres, pages 22–31,
Valencia, Spain, April 3, 2017.

nodes standing for sentences and weighted edges representing a distance between sentences. Conroy et al. (2005) presented the CLASSY summarizer that used a hidden Markov model based on signature terms and query terms for sentence selection within a document, and a pivoted question answering algorithm for redundancy removal. Liu et al. (2012) proposed QS with multi-document input using unsupervised deep learning. Schilder and Kondadadi (2008) presented FastSum - a fast query-based multi-document summarizer based solely on word-frequency features of clusters, documents, and topics, where summary sentences are ranked by a regression support vector machine. Tang et al. (2009) proposed two strategies to incorporate the query information into a probabilistic model. Park et al. (2006) introduced a method that uses non-negative matrix factorization to extract query-relevant sentences. Some works deal with domain-specific data (Chen and Verma, 2006) and use domain-specific terms when measuring the distance between sentences and a query. Zhou et al. (2006) describes a query-based multi-document summarizer based on basic elements, a head-modifier-relation triple representation of document content. Recently, many works integrate topic modeling into their summarization models. For example, Li and Li (2014) extend the standard graph ranking algorithm by proposing a two-layer (sentence layer and topic layer) graph-based semi-supervised learning approach based on topic modeling techniques. Wang et al. (2014) present a submodular function-based framework for query-focused opinion summarization. Within their framework, relevance ordering produced by a statistical ranker, and information coverage with respect to topic distribution and diverse viewpoints are both encoded as submodular functions. Some works (Li et al., 2015) use external resources with the goal to better represent the importance of a text unit and its semantic similarity with the given query. Otterbacher et al. (2009) present Biased LexRank method, which represents a text as a graph of passages linked based on their pairwise lexical similarity, identifies passages that are likely to be relevant to a users natural language question and then perform a random walk on the lexical similarity graph in order to recursively retrieve additional passages that are similar relevant passages. Williams et al. (2014) provides a task-based evaluation of multiple query biased summarization methods for cross-language information retrieval using relevance prediction. In (Litvak et al., 2015) we applied the MDL principle to generic summarization, where we considered frequent word sets as the means for encoding text. The results demonstrated superiority of the proposed method over other methods on DUC data. This paper continues the above work by constructing a model where frequent word sets depend on the query.

3 Methodology

3.1 Overview

Our approach consists of the following steps: (1) text preprocessing, (2) query-related frequent itemset mining, (3) finding the best MDL model, and (4) sentence ranking for the summary construction. The general scheme of our approach is depicted in Figure 1. Details of every step are given in sections below. Section 3.8 contains an example of intermediate and the final (the summary) outputs for one of the document clusters from DUC 2005 dataset.

3.2 Query-based MDL principle

The Minimum Description Length (MDL) Principle is based on the idea that a regularity in the data can be used to compress the data, and this compression should use fewer symbols than the data itself. Intuitively, a *model* is a partial function from data subsets to codes, where the codes size has logarithmic growth.

In general, given a set of models $\mathcal{M}$, a model $M \in \mathcal{M}$ is considered the *best* if it minimizes $L(M) + L(D|M)$, where $L(M)$ is the bit length of description of M and $L(D|M)$ is the bit length of the dataset D encoded with M. As such, the frequency and the length of the codes that replace data subsets are the most important features of the MDL model. Because we aim at query-based summarization, in our approach we seek a query-dependent model M_Q that minimizes $L(M_Q) + L(D|M_Q)$; it may not be the best model overall but it has to be the best among models for the query Q. Note that the MDL approach does not use the actual codes but only takes into account their bit size.

3.3 Query-based data setup

In our case both text and query undergo preprocessing that includes sentence splitting, tokeniza-

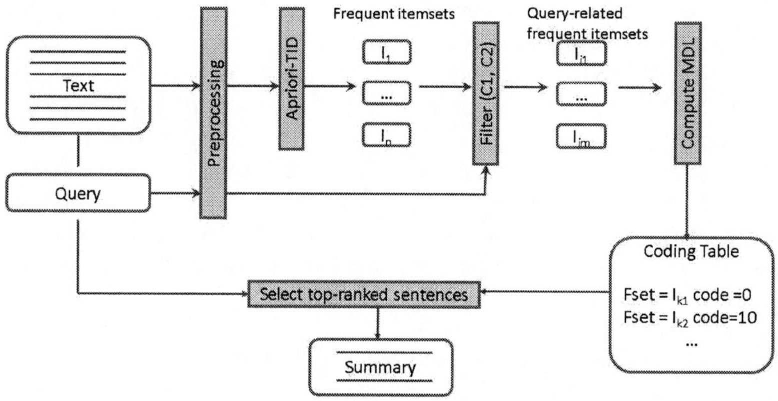

Figure 1: Query-based MDL summarization

tion, stemming, and stop-words removal. Additionally, sentences that are too long (over 40 words), too short (less than 5 words), or consist primarily of direct speech (main portion of a sentence is contained within quotes), are omitted. The number of these sentences is small and we noted that their inclusion in summaries, although rare, decreases summary quality. No deep linguistic analysis is performed, and therefore this method is suitable for any language with basic tools.

A query is considered to be a set of stemmed tokens, e.g., terms, even if it contains more than one sentence. A document or a document set (in case of multi-document summarization) D is treated as a dataset where each sentence is a *transaction* that is a set of stemmed tokens. The order of words in a sentence is ignored in our model, because we consider the relation of a sentence to a query to be more important than the order in which a sentence utilizes query tokens. Formally, we have sentences $S_1, \dots, S_n$ of a document set where every sentence is a subset of unique terms (stemmed tokens), denoted by $T_1, \dots, T_m$. A query Q is a subset of unique terms as well.

3.4 Frequent itemsets

In our approach, we refer to text as a transactional dataset, where each sentence is considered to be a single *transaction* consisting of *items*. An item in our case is a term, i.e. stemmed word. Therefore, a sentence is viewed as a set of terms contained in it. A set of items, called an *itemset*, is *frequent* if it is contained (as a set) in S sentences, where $S \geq 1$ is user-defined parameter.

The paper (Agrawal and Srikant, 1994) has proposed two algorithms–Apriori and Apriori-TID–for processing large databases and mining frequent itemsets in efficient time. The Apriori algorithm makes multiple passes over the database while Apriori-TID algorithm uses the database only once, in the first pass. In this work, we use the Apriori-TID algorithm for frequent itemset mining. While multitude of algorithms performing the same task exist, Apriori-TID is sufficient for our purposes because texts, treated as transactional datasets, are rarely dense, and therefore the number of frequent itemsets found in texts is usually not very large.

3.5 Data encoding

In general MDL approach, a *Coding Table* is a collection CT of sets from D that are used as a model of our dataset. According to the MDL principle, CT is considered to be the *best* when it minimizes encoded dataset size $size(D, CT) = L(CT) + L(D|CT)$. In general MDL approach, a *Coding Table* is a collection CT of sets from D that are used as a model of our dataset. According to the MDL principle, CT is considered to be the *best* when it minimizes encoded dataset size $size(D, CT) = L(CT) + L(D|CT)$.

In our approach, sets included in the Coding Table come from the set F of all frequent word sets in our text. Moreover, we only keep a frequent set in F if it is query-related, and therefore all the sets in CT are query-related as well. Every member $I \in CT$ is associated with its $code(I)$ of logarithmic growth (for instance, prefix codes may be used). In our case, the choice of a specific code is not important as we only use its size $|code(I)|$ when computing $size(D, CT)$. We use Huffman Coding in the current version, where $|code(I)| = \log |I|$. General approach of using frequent sets for dataset MDL representation first appeared in (Vreeken et al., 2011); here, we apply it to text and only care about word sets related to a query.

There are two main orders to consider: Standard Candidate Order in which F is kept, whose purpose is to build the coding table faster. Itemsets in F are first sorted by increasing support, then by decreasing sequence length, then lexicographically. The Standard Cover Order of CT keeps its members sorted by first by decreasing sequence length, then by decreasing support, and finally, in lexicographical order. Using this order ensures that encoding of the dataset with CT indeed produces minimal encoding length $L(D|CT)$ for fixed CT. Validity of this approach is proven in (Vreeken et al., 2011).

3.6 Sentence ranking and summary construction

We are interested in the dataset $D|CT$ after it is compressed in the best possible way with the best compressing query-related set CT. The dataset $D|CT$ is obtained by replacing in D every itemset in CT by its code, and shorter codes are selected first. We use an upper bound on the size of CT, in order to limit document compression, and select it to be *equal to the target summary size*, which is denoted by *SummarySize*. The ideal compression in this case will compress only words most relevant to the summary and will ignore everything else; additionally, this limitation speeds up computation.

The summary is constructed by iteratively selecting the sentences according to the coverage of CT. At each step, a sentence that covers the most important uncovered itemset in CT is added to a summary. Importance of itemsets in CT is determined by their order – higher itemsets in CT (those with shorter codes) have higher importance.

3.7 Query-based frequent itemsets and data encoding

In order to direct the summarization process towards the given query, we compute and use for encoding only frequent itemsets that are related to the given query. We tested two different types of constraints on frequent itemsets:

- **(C1)** All terms in a frequent itemset I must be contained in the query: $I \subseteq Q$.
  With this approach, a set of words in a sentence is encoded only if these words appear in the query.
- **(C2)** Every frequent itemset and the query must have a common term: $I \cap Q \neq \emptyset$.
  Here, a set of words in a sentence is encoded if at least one word in the set appears in the query.

Both methods ensure that only terms related to the query are taken into account. Therefore, instead of all frequent itemsets F, we only use its subset $F_{Ci}, i = 1, 2$. The general Standard Candidate Order is used, and members of F_{Ci} are sorted by by increasing support, then by decreasing sequence length, then lexicographically.

Because the coding table CT can now contain members of F_{Ci} only, we modify the Standard Cover Order of CT accordingly in order to compress query-related terms first. The order is modified as follows:

- **(C1)** Because every member of CT contains *only* terms used in the query, we sort it first by decreasing sequence length, then by increasing support, and then lexicographically. Here, sequence length is precisely the number of query terms contained in a frequent itemset, and itemsets containing more query terms get higher priority.
- **(C2)** Every member of CT has *some* common terms with the query, we sort CT first by the number of terms common to an itemset and the query, then by decreasing sequence length, then by increasing support, and then lexicographically. Here, a precedence is given to itemsets that have more in common to the query. Note that we tested other measures for distance between itemsets and the query (Jaccard similarity, cosine similarity), but this method provided better results.

Detailed description of our query-based summarization method Qump (Query-based Krimp) is given in Algorithm 1.

3.8 Example

Here we demonstrate intermediate and the final (summary) outputs for the document cluster

Algorithm 1: Qump: Query-Based Krimp

Input:

(1) a document or a document set D, preprocessed as in Section 3.3,
(2) a query Q preprocessed as in Section 3.3,
(3) target summary word limit *SummarySize*,
(4) support bound **S**,
(5) constraint **Cx** on frequent itemsets as described in Section 3.7.

Output: Extractive summary $Summary$

```
/* STEP 1: Query-related frequent set mining */
(1a) F ← frequent sets of terms from {T_1, ..., T_m}
  appearing in at least Supp fraction of sentences that
  satisfy constraint Cx;
(1b) Sort F according to Standard Candidate Order;
/* STEP 2: Initialize the coding table */
(2a) Add all terms T_1, ..., T_m and their support to
  CT;
(2b) Keep CT always sorted according to Standard
  Cover Order;
(2c) Initialize prefix codes according to the order of
  sets in CT;
/* STEP 3: Find the best encoding */
(3a) EncodedData ←
  PrefixEncoding({S_1, ..., S_n}, CT);
(3b) CodeCount ← 0;
while CodeCount < SummarySize and F ≠ ∅ do
  | BestCode ← arg min_{c∈F} L(CT ∪ {c}) +
  |   L(PrefixEncoding({S_1, ..., S_n}, CT ∪ {c}));
  | CT ← CT ∪ {BestCode};
  | F ← F \ {BestCode};
  | /* If a code is used, its supercodes cannot
  |  appear in the data */
  | F ← F \ {d ∈ F | BestCode ⊂ d};
  | CodeCount++;
end
/* STEP 4: Build the summary */
Summary ← ∅;
for codes c ∈ CT do
  | importance(c) := serial number of c in CT
end
while |Summary| < SummarySize do
  | for all unselected sentences S do
  |   | nCov(S) ← Σ_{c∈CT} importance(c)/|S|
  | end
  | S ← arg max_S nCov(S);
  | Summary ← Summary ∪ {S};
  | CT := CT \ {c}
  | for d ⊂ c do
  |   | CT := CT \ {d}
  | end
end
return Summary
```

D301I and the query *"International Organized Crime Identify and describe types of organized crime that crosses borders or involves more than one country. Name the countries involved. Also identify the perpetrators involved with each type of crime, including both individuals and organizations if possible."* from the DUC 2005 dataset.

- The coding table CT (only its top 8 itemsets with the shortest codes, sorted from the most important to the least) is given in Table 1.

Code #	Itemset
0	cross border
1	countri includ
2	crime countri
3	border cross
4	countri identifi
5	drug
6	cocain
7	offici
...	...

Table 1: CT example, top records.

- The sentence *"The drugs organisation used intricate methods - including bank accounts, couriers and ships as well as dummy and real companies in many countries - to smuggle cocaine from South America to Europe."* after encoding (replacement of phrases by codes) looks like this: *"code#5 code#24 intric method includ code#19 account courier ship dummi real compani mani code#16 code#23 code#6 south america code#40"*, and it covers 7 out of 50 codes from the CT. Normalized by the sentence length, its coverage is the largest among all sentences, and therefore it is selected to the summary.

- The summary contains 8 following sentences with the highest CT coverage, ordered by their appearance in the summarized documents:
"The drugs organization used intricate methods - including bank accounts, couriers and ships as well as dummy and real companies in many countries - to smuggle cocaine from South America to Europe. But this week the New York Times gave extensive coverage to a report from a US intelligence officer that warned Mexican drug-traffickers were planning to take advantage of lax border controls. The measures announced yesterday include a CDollars 5 tax cut per carton of cigarettes, bringing federal taxes down to CDollars 11 a carton. Mr Louis Freeh, the FBI director who arrived in Moscow yesterday as part of a central and East European tour, said the mounting crime wave in Russia posed 'common threats' to all. Crime Without Frontiers

is the story of how western and eastern criminal syndicates secured the former Soviet safehouse, the last piece in constructing a global pax mafiosa. In the pax mafiosa, business is business - the Chinese Triads are partners in crime with the American Mafia; the Italians use the Russians to launder for the Colombian cartels, the Japanese Yakuza work hand in hand with the Italians. Last January, after the ouster of Panamanian strongman Manuel A. Noriega, the new government of Panama agreed to U.S. requests for records of bank accounts identified as having been used by cartel money launderers. Cuba's interior minister, the Cabinet officer in charge of domestic law enforcement, was fired Thursday as that nation's drug purge continued, but the crackdown has failed to touch other leaders who U.S. officials say are involved in trafficking."

4 Experiments

4.1 Dataset

We selected two English corpora of the Document Understanding Conference (DUC): DUC 2006 and DUC 2005 (DUC, 2005 2006) for our experiments, which are standard datasets used for query-based summarization methods evaluation.

The DUC 2005 dataset contains 50 documents sets of 25-50 related documents each. Average number of words in a document set is 20185. For every document set a short (1-3 sentences) query is supplied. From 4 to 9 gold standard summaries are supplied for every document set, and the target summary size is 250 words.

The DUC 2006 dataset contains 50 documents sets of 25 related document each. Average number of words in a document set is 15293. For every document set a short (1-3 sentences) query is supplied. Four gold standard summaries are supplied for every document set, and the target summary size is 250 words.

4.2 Experiment setup

We generated summaries for each set of related documents (by considering each set of documents as one meta-document) in the DUC 2005 and DUC 2006 corpora. The summarization quality was measured by the ROUGE-1 (Lin, 2004) recall scores[1] , with the word limit set to 250, without stemming and stopword removal. We limited the size of the coding table by 250, as described in Section 3.4, and set support count $\mathbf{S} = 2$ in order to take into account all terms repeated twice or more in the text.

4.3 Results

Table 2 shows the ROUGE-1 scores of our algorithm comparative to the scores of 32 systems that participated in the DUC 2005 competition. Two options of our algorithm that correspond to constraints described in Section 3.7 appear in the "Systems" column of Table 2, denoted by Qump(C1-C2). Qump(C2) places third on the ROUGE-1 recall and f-measure, and the difference between the top systems (ID=15 and ID=4) and our algorithm is statistically insignificant.

System 15 stands for the NUS summarizer from the National University of Singapore. This summarizer is based on the concept link approach (Ye et al., 2005). NUS method uses two features: sentence semantic similarity and redundancy minimization based on Maximal Marginal Relevance (MMR). The first one is computed as an overall similarity score between each sentence and the remainder of the document cluster. This overall similarity score reflects the strength of representative power of the sentence in regard to the rest of the document cluster and is used as the primary sentence ranking metric while forming the summary. Then, a module similar to MMR is employed to build the summary incrementally, minimizing redundancy and maintaining the summarys relevance to the query's topic. In order to reduce the run-time computational cost (required for a scan through all possible pairs of senses for all pairs of concepts), authors pre-computed the semantic similarity between all possible pairs of WordNet entries offline.

System 4 represents the Columbia summarizer from the Columbia University (Blair-Goldensohn, 2005). This is an adaptation of the DefScriber question answering (QA) system (Blair-Goldensohn et al., 2004). DefScriber (1) identifies relevant sentences which contain information pertinent to the target individual or term (i.e. the X in the "Who/What is X?" question); (2) incrementally clusters extracted sentences using a cosine

[1] we used ROUGE-1.5.5 version and the command line "-a -l 250 -n 2 -2 4 -u"

distance metric; then (3) selects sentences for output summary using a fitness function which maximizes inclusion of core definitional predicates, coverage of the highest ranking clusters, and answer cohesion; and finally (4) applies reference rewriting techniques to extracted sentences to improve readability of summary, using an auxiliary system (Nenkova and McKeown, 2003). The key adaptations made for the DUC 2005 task were in relevant-passage selection (step 1) by combining the following techniques:

1. Term frequency-based weighting for filtering the less relevant terms from the topic statement ("topic terms"), based on IDF calculated over a large news corpus;

2. Topic structure for adjustment the topic term weights with the simple heuristic of giving terms in the title double the weight of terms in the extended question/topic body;

3. Stemming for maximize coverage of relevant terms when measuring overlap of topic terms and document sentences;

4. Including content of the nearby-sentences in the determination of a given sentences relevance.

Using these techniques, the algorithm made two passes over each document. In the first pass assigning relevance scores to each sentence based on overlap with topic terms. In the second pass, these scores were adjusted using the first-pass scores of nearby sentences. Finally, the sentences scored above a certain cutoff were selected.

In comparison to the two top systems, our approach does not require any pre-computed data from the external resources (like NUS does), and has a very simple pipeline with a few stages (unlike the Columbia summarizer) which do not involve external tools and have a low computational cost.

The difference of Qump(C2) from system with ID=17 was statistically insignificant, and the difference from system with ID=11 was statistically significant.

Table 3 shows how the ROUGE-1 scores of our algorithm compare to the scores of 35 systems that participated in the DUC 2006 competition. Two options of our algorithm that correspond to constraints described in Section 3.7 appear in the table, denoted by Qump(C1-C2). Qump(C2) places

System ID	Recall	Precision	F-measure
15	0.3446	0.3436	0.3440
4	0.3424	0.3355	0.3388
Qump(C2)	0.3416	0.3334	0.3374
17	0.3400	0.3329	0.3363
11	0.3336	0.3134	0.3231
6	0.3310	0.3256	0.3282
19	0.3305	0.3249	0.3276
10	0.3304	0.3225	0.3263
7	0.3300	0.3211	0.3254
8	0.3292	0.3314	0.3301
5	0.3281	0.3406	0.3339
Qump(C1)	0.3276	0.3194	0.3233
25	0.3264	0.3197	0.3229
24	0.3223	0.3253	0.3237
9	0.3222	0.3138	0.3179
16	0.3209	0.3203	0.3205
3	0.3177	0.3179	0.3177
14	0.3172	0.3325	0.3235
12	0.3115	0.3043	0.3078
21	0.3107	0.3095	0.3100
29	0.3107	0.3159	0.3131
27	0.3069	0.2976	0.3021
28	0.3047	0.3074	0.3059
13	0.3039	0.3186	0.3109
18	0.3003	0.3350	0.3161
32	0.2977	0.3056	0.3014
30	0.2931	0.2900	0.2914
26	0.2824	0.3088	0.2949
2	0.2801	0.3052	0.2914
22	0.2795	0.3160	0.2878
31	0.2719	0.3062	0.2797
20	0.2552	0.3554	0.2930
1	0.2532	0.3104	0.2644
23	0.1647	0.3708	0.2196

Table 2: DUC 2005. ROUGE-1 scores.

second on the ROUGE-1 recall and f-measure, and the difference between the top system with ID=24 and our algorithm is statistically insignificant.

ID 24 represents the IIITH-Sum system from the International Institute of Information Technology (Jagarlamudi et al., 2006). IIITH-Sum used two features to score the sentences, and then picked the top-scored ones to a summary in the greedy manner. The first feature is a query dependent adaptation of the HAL (Jagadeesh et al., 2005) feature, where an additional importance is given to a word/phrase of a query. The second feature calculates query-independent sentence importance, using external resources in the web. First, the Yahoo search engine was used to get a ranked list of retrieved documents, and a unigram language model was learned on a text content extracted from them. Then, Information Measure (IM), using entropy to compute the information content of a sentence based on the learned unigram model, was used for scoring a sentence. The final sentence ranks were computed as a weighted linear combination of modified HAL feature and IM.

In contrast to the IIIHT-Sum, our approach does not require any external resources and is strictly based on the internal content of the analyzed corpus. As results, it is also consumes less run-time.

The difference of Qump(C2) from system with

System ID	Recall	Precision	F-measure
24	0.3797	0.3781	0.3789
Qump(C2)	0.3745	0.3732	0.3745
12	0.3736	0.3734	0.3734
31	0.3675	0.3730	0.3702
10	0.3720	0.3680	0.3699
33	0.3700	0.3698	0.3699
15	0.3717	0.3675	0.3696
23	0.3726	0.3661	0.3692
28	0.3677	0.3707	0.3691
8	0.3702	0.3665	0.3683
27	0.3574	0.3707	0.3637
5	0.3665	0.3607	0.3635
Qump(C1)	0.3647	0.3623	0.3635
13	0.3553	0.3713	0.3629
3	0.3539	0.3650	0.3593
2	0.3587	0.3580	0.3583
6	0.3543	0.3567	0.3555
19	0.3552	0.3534	0.3542
4	0.3518	0.3567	0.3542
22	0.3518	0.3554	0.3536
29	0.3432	0.3598	0.3512
9	0.3373	0.3641	0.3492
32	0.3519	0.3466	0.3492
14	0.3501	0.3481	0.3490
30	0.3317	0.3575	0.3439
25	0.3374	0.3478	0.3425
20	0.3413	0.3412	0.3412
7	0.3417	0.3368	0.3392
16	0.3384	0.3377	0.3380
18	0.3335	0.3423	0.3377
17	0.3105	0.3647	0.3351
21	0.3244	0.3541	0.3344
34	0.3320	0.3300	0.3310
35	0.3058	0.3488	0.3242
26	0.3023	0.3399	0.3199
1	0.2789	0.3231	0.2962
11	0.1965	0.3014	0.2366

Table 3: DUC 2006. ROUGE-1 scores.

ID=12 was statistically insignificant, and the difference from system with ID=31 was statistically significant. It is not surprising that method C2 performed better that C1 as limiting frequent word sets to words appearing in a query only decreases the overall number of frequent word sets. In this case, many repetitive word sets that are related to the query are missed.

The actual running time of our Qump (both versions) was around 1-3 seconds per document sets. We also learned that long sentences do not affect computation cost of our approach.

5 Conclusions

This work introduces Qump, a system following a new MDL-based approach to a query-oriented summarization. Qump extracts sentences that best describe the query-related frequent set of words. The evaluation results show that Qump has an excellent performance. In absolute ranking, it outperforms all but two of participated systems in DUC 2005 competition and all but one of competing systems in DUC 2006 contest. According to significance test, Qump has the same performance as leading systems in both competitions (ID=15,4,7 in DUC-2005 and ID=24,12 in DUC-2006). In addition, Qump is an efficient algorithm having polynomial complexity. Qump's runtime is limited by Apriori that is known as a PSPACE-complete problem. However, because it is a rare occasion to have a set of words repeated in more than 4-5 different sentences in the entire document set, we have $O(n^5)$ frequent itemsets at most where n is the number of terms. The encoding process is bound by a number of frequent sets times a number of sentences (m) times a number of words (k). Therefore, we can say that Qump's runtime is polynomial in the number of terms and is bound by $O(m \times k \times n^5)$. In conclusion, the presented technique has the following advantages over other techniques: (1) It is unsupervised and does not require any external resources (many of the top-rated systems from the DUC competitions are supervised or use external data); (2) It has efficient time complexity (polynomial in the number of terms); (3) It is language-independent and can be applied on any language, as far as we have a tokenizer for this language (for example, we got excellent results with generic summarization in Chinese with this approach[2]); (4) Despite its robustness (independence on annotated data and language, and its efficiency), its performance is comparable to the one of the top systems.

In future, we intend to enrich this approach with word vectors for better match between a query and a sentence. Also, we plan to integrate it with a novel summarization technique using OLAP representation, where frequent itemsets of words will represent an additional dimension.

References

Rakesh Agrawal and Ramakrishnan Srikant. 1994. Fast algorithms for mining association rules. In *20th International Conference on Very Large Databases*, pages 487–499.

Sasha Blair-Goldensohn, Kathleen McKeown, and Andrew H. Schlaikjer, 2004. *Answering definitional questions: A hybrid approach*, chapter 4. AAAI Press.

Sasha Blair-Goldensohn. 2005. From definitions to complex topics: Columbia university at DUC 2005. In *Document Understanding Conference*.

Wauter Bosma, 2005. *Query-Based Summarization using Rhetorical Structure Theory*, pages 29–44. LOT.

[2] Litvak, M. and Vanetik, N. and Li, L., 2017, *Summarizing Weibo with Topics Compression*, unpublished manuscript.

Shaofeng Bu, Laks V. S. Lakshmanan, and Raymond T. Ng. 2005. Mdl summarization with holes. In *Proceedings of the 31st International Conference on Very Large Data Bases*, VLDB '05, pages 433–444.

Ping Chen and Rakesh Verma. 2006. A query-based medical information summarization system using ontology knowledge. In *Proceedings of the 19th IEEE Symposium on Computer-Based Medical Systems (CBMS06)*, pages 37–42.

John M. Conroy, Judith D. Schlesinger, and Jade Goldstein Stewart. 2005. CLASSY: Query-based multi-document summarization. In *DUC 05 Conference Proceedings*.

Hal Daumé III and Daniel Marcu. 2006. Bayesian query-focused summarization. In *Proceedings of the 21st International Conference on Computational Linguistics and 44th Annual Meeting of the Association for Computational Linguistics*, pages 305–312, Sydney, Australia, July. Association for Computational Linguistics.

DUC. 2005-2006. Document Understanding Conference. `http://duc.nist.gov`.

Jagarlamudi Jagadeesh, Prasad Pingali, and Vasudeva Varma. 2005. A relevance-based language modeling approach to DUC 2005. In *Document Understanding Conferences (along with HLT-EMNLP 2005)*.

Jagadeesh Jagarlamudi, Prasad Pingali, and Vasudeva Varma. 2006. Query independent sentence scoring approach to DUC 2006.

Laks V. S. Lakshmanan, Raymond T. Ng, Christine Xing Wang, Xiaodong Zhou, and Theodore J. Johnson. 2002. The generalized mdl approach for summarization. In *Proceedings of the 28th International Conference on Very Large Data Bases*, VLDB '02, pages 766–777.

Yanran Li and Sujian Li. 2014. Query-focused multi-document summarization: Combining a topic model with graph-based semi-supervised learning. In *Proceedings of COLING 2014, the 25th International Conference on Computational Linguistics: Technical Papers*, pages 1197–1207, Dublin, Ireland, August. Dublin City University and Association for Computational Linguistics.

Chen Li, Yang Liu, and Lin Zhao. 2015. Using external resources and joint learning for bigram weighting in ilp-based multi-document summarization. In *Proceedings of the 2015 Conference of the North American Chapter of the Association for Computational Linguistics: Human Language Technologies*, pages 778–787, Denver, Colorado, May–June. Association for Computational Linguistics.

Chin-Yew Lin. 2004. ROUGE: A Package for Automatic Evaluation of summaries. In *Proceedings of the Workshop on Text Summarization Branches Out (WAS 2004)*, pages 25–26.

Marina Litvak, Mark Last, and Natalia Vanetik. 2015. Krimping texts for better summarization. In *Proceedings of the 2015 Conference on Empirical Methods in Natural Language Processing*, pages 1931–1935, Lisbon, Portugal, September. Association for Computational Linguistics.

Yan Liu, Sheng hua Zhong, and Wenjie Li. 2012. Query-oriented multi-document summarization via unsupervised deep learning. In *Proceedings of the Twenty-Sixth AAAI conference on Artificial Intelligence*, pages 1699–1705.

Ahmed A. Mohamed and Sanguthevar Rajasekaran. 2006. Query-based summarization based on document graphs. In *Proceedings of IEEE International Symposium on Signal Processing and Information Technology*, pages 408–410.

Ani Nenkova and Kathleen McKeown. 2003. References to named entities: a corpus study. In *NAACL-HLT 2003*.

Thanh-Son Nguyen, Hady W. Lauw, and Panayiotis Tsaparas. 2015. Review synthesis for micro-review summarization. In *Proceedings of the Eighth ACM International Conference on Web Search and Data Mining*, WSDM'15, pages 169–178.

Tadashi Nomoto and Yuji Matsumoto. 2001. A new approach to unsupervised text summarization. In *Proceedings of the 24th Annual International ACM SIGIR Conference on Research and Development in Information Retrieval*, SIGIR '01, pages 26–34.

Tadashi Nomoto. 2004. *Machine Learning Approaches to Rhetorical Parsing and Open-Domain Text Summarization*. Ph.D. thesis, Nara Institute of Science and Technology.

Jahna Otterbacher, Gunes Erkan, and Dragomir R. Radev. 2009. Biased lexrank: Passage retrieval using random walks with question-based priors. *Information Processing & Management*, 45(1):42–54.

Sun Park, Ju-Hong Lee, Chan-Min Ahn, Jun Sik Hong, and Seok-Ju Chun, 2006. *Query Based Summarization Using Non-negative Matrix Factorization*, volume 4253 of *Lecture Notes in Computer Science*, pages 84–89.

Frank Schilder and Ravikumar Kondadadi. 2008. Fastsum: Fast and accurate query-based multi-document summarization. In *Proceedings of ACL-08: HLT, Short Papers*, pages 205–208, Columbus, Ohio, June. Association for Computational Linguistics.

Jie Tang, Limin Yao, and Dewei Chen. 2009. Multi-topic based query-oriented summarization. In *SIAM International Conference Data Mining*.

Jilles Vreeken, Matthijs Leeuwen, and Arno Siebes. 2011. Krimp: Mining itemsets that compress. *Data Min. Knowl. Discov.*, 23(1):169–214, July.

Lu Wang, Hema Raghavan, Claire Cardie, and Vittorio Castelli. 2014. Query-focused opinion summarization for user-generated content. In *Proceedings of COLING 2014, the 25th International Conference on Computational Linguistics: Technical Papers*, pages 1660–1669, Dublin, Ireland, August. Dublin City University and Association for Computational Linguistics.

Jennifer Williams, Sharon Tam, and Wade Shen. 2014. Finding good enough: A task-based evaluation of query biased summarization for cross-language information retrieval. In *Proceedings of the 2014 Conference on Empirical Methods in Natural Language Processing (EMNLP)*, pages 657–669, Doha, Qatar, October. Association for Computational Linguistics.

Shiren Ye, Long Qiu, Tat-Seng Chua, and Min-Yen Kan. 2005. NUS at DUC 2005: understanding documents via concept links. In *Document Understanding Conference*.

Liang Zhou, Chin-Yew, and Eduard Hovy. 2006. Summarizing answers for complicated questions. In *Proceedings of the Fifth International Conference on Language Resources and Evaluation (LREC-2006)*.

Word Embedding and Topic Modeling Enhanced Multiple Features for Content Linking and Argument/Sentiment Labeling in Online Forums

Lei Li and **Liyuan Mao** and **Moye Chen**
Center for Intelligence Science and Technology (CIST)
School of Computer Science
Beijing University of Posts and Telecommunications (BUPT) , China
leili@bupt.edu.cn circleyuan@bupt.edu.cn moyec@bupt.edu.cn

Abstract

Multiple grammatical and semantic features are adopted in content linking and argument/sentiment labeling for online forums in this paper. There are mainly two different methods for content linking. First, we utilize the deep feature obtained from Word Embedding Model in deep learning and compute sentence similarity. Second, we use multiple traditional features to locate candidate linking sentences, and then adopt a voting method to obtain the final result. LDA topic modeling is used to mine latent semantic feature and K-means clustering is implemented for argument labeling, while features from sentiment dictionaries and rule-based sentiment analysis are integrated for sentiment labeling. Experimental results have shown that our methods are valid.

1 Introduction

Comments to news and their providers in online forums have been increasing rapidly in recent years with a large number of user participants and huge amount of interactive contents. How can we understand the mass of comments effectively? A crucial initial step towards this goal should be content linking, which is to determine what comments link to, be that either specific news snippets or comments by other users. Furthermore, a set of labels for a given link may be articulated to capture phenomena such as agreement and sentiment with respect to the comment target.

Content linking is a relatively new research topic and it has attracted the focus of TAC 2014 (https://tac.nist.gov//2014/KBP/), BIRNDL 2016 (Jaidka et al., 2016) and MultiLing 2015 (Kabadjov et al., 2015) and MultiLing 2017. The main method is based on the calculation of sentence similarity (Aggarwal and Sharma, 2016; Cao et al., 2016; Jaidka et al., 2016; Saggion et al., 2016; Nomoto, 2016; Moraes et al., 2016; Malenfant and Lapalme, 2016; Lu et al., 2016; Li et al., 2016; Klampfl et al., 2016), with the key point of mining semantic information better.

Researchers have tried various features and methods for sentiment and argument labeling. The main features are different kinds of sentiment dictionaries, while the basic method is the rule-based one. The major method for sentiment and argument labeling is based on statistical machine learning algorithms (Aker et al., 2015; Hristo Tanev, 2015; Maynard and Funk, 2011).

2 Task Description

We work on three tasks for English and Italian in this paper. The first one is content linking, which is to find all the linking pairs for comment sentences. In every pair, one sentence belongs to the original article or a former comment by an author, the other belongs to a comment by a later commentator. The second and third tasks are to tag two kinds of labels to the linking pairs that were found in the first task. Labels involve argument label and sentiment label. For argument label, it focuses on whether or not a commentator agrees with the commentated author. For sentiment label, it cares about the sentiment of comment sentences. Experiments are implemented on the training data released by MultiLing 2017, including 20 English news (from The Guardian) and 5 Italian (from Le Monde) news with some comments.

3 Methods

For content linking, we adopt the Word Embedding Model to dig up word vectors as linking information of sentence pair with deeper semantic fea-

Proceedings of the MultiLing 2017 Workshop on Summarization and Summary Evaluation Across Source Types and Genres, pages 32–36,
Valencia, Spain, April 3, 2017.

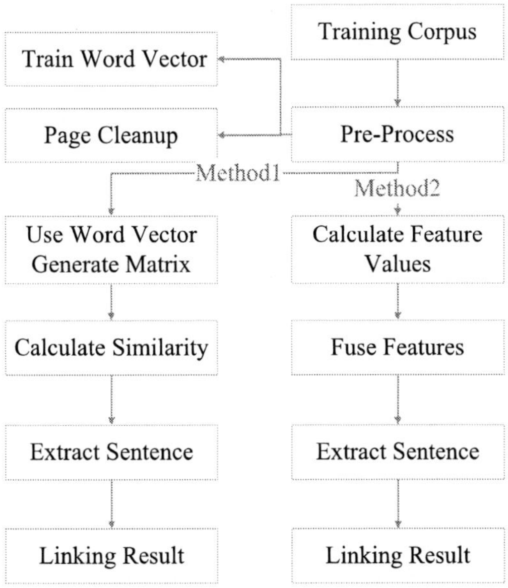

Figure 1: Content linking process

tures. Besides, we also use some traditional features of sentence similarity which performed well through experiments and explore how to fuse them together with Word Embedding features. For this purpose, first, we try to use every single feature to get one linking sentence, next, we choose the most repetitive sentence as final result via a voting method. Then we mainly use rule-based sentiment analysis to obtain the sentiment label. LDA (Latent Dirichlet Allocation) (Blei et al., 2003) topic model and K-means (Hartigan and Wong, 1979) are integrated to obtain the argument label.

3.1 Content Linking

Figure 1 shows the process for content linking.

3.1.1 Pre-Processing

We crawl 1.5G data from the English Guardian website to train word vectors for English, and about 1G data from Wikipedia for Italian. Then we use the tool named word2vec (Mikolov et al., 2013) for training.

3.1.2 Method 1-Word Vector Algorithm

After the training of word embedding models, a sentence in the corpus can be expressed as:

$$W_t = (w_t, w_{t+1}, \cdots, w_{t+k}) \tag{1}$$

Where w_t is the word vector of 300 dimensions of word t. Then two sentences W_i and W_j can form a calculating matrix $M_{i,j}$:

$$M_{i,j} = W_i W_j^T = \begin{bmatrix} w_t w_v & \cdots & w_t w_{v+l} \\ \vdots & \ddots & \vdots \\ w_{t+k} w_v & \cdots & w_{t+k} w_{v+l} \end{bmatrix} \tag{2}$$

Before the computation of (w_t, w_v), we need some processing steps: stemming as well as stop words and punctuation removing. Besides, it is essential to check relations between word t and word v based on WordNet. If they exist in the hyponyms/hypernyms part of each other, they can be seen as the same.

The cosine distance can represent (w_t, w_v), and the similarity of sentences i and j is:

$$Sim_{i,j} = \frac{\sum_{m=i,n=j} max(M_{m,n})}{\sqrt{length_i length_j}} \tag{3}$$

Where $maxM_{m,n}$ is obtained through the following concrete steps. First, find out the maximum of $M_{i,j}$, then delete the row and column of the maximum. Next, find the maximum of the remaining matrix and remove row and column like the former step. Do the same procedure until the matrix is empty. Finally add up all the maximum values. $length_i$ is the number of word vectors in the sentence, and $\sqrt{length_i length_j}$ is used to reduce the influence of sentence length.

We think that the maximum value in the matrix can represent the most matching word pairs in the two sentences. We just choose the maximum value in each step and delete the word pairs in the matrix for next iteration until the matrix is empty. As a result, we can find out all the best matching word pairs in the two sentences. Hence accumulation of word similarities of all these best matching word pairs can represent the similarities of the two sentences.

Based on the above sentence similarities, we can extract those sentences with the highest similarity to a comment sentence as its linking result.

3.1.3 Method 2-Feature Fusion Algorithm

This algorithm is only for English. We have two kinds of features, one is from lexicons, and the other is from sentence similarities.

We have three lexicons: Linked Text high-frequency word lexicon (Lexicon 1), LDA lexicon (Lexicon 2), Comment Text and Linked Text co-occurrence lexicon (Lexicon 3). For Lexicon 1, we pick up the words with high frequency from standard answers artificially, and then expand them

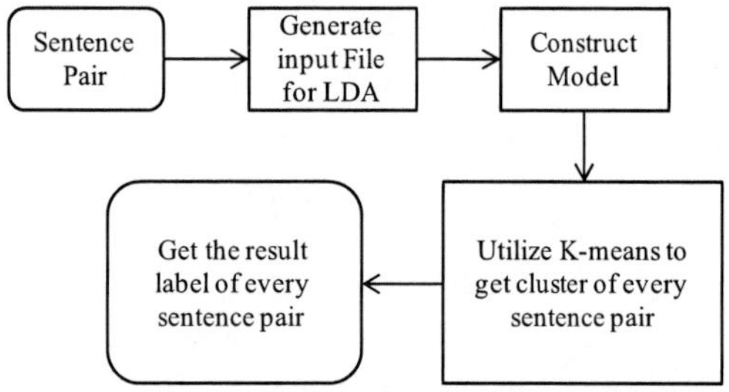

Figure 2: Argument label process

through WordNet and word vectors, resulting in a lexicon. For Lexicon 2, we use LDA model to train the news and comments to get a lexicon of 25 latent topics in every file independently. For Lexicon 3, we obtain the co-occurrence degree between words by the word frequency statistics of comment and its linked sentence from the training corpus.

As for sentence similarities, we have word vector similarity, jaccard similarity, idf similarity, res similarity, jcn similarity and path similarity. Word vector similarity is calculated through Method 1. We add up the idf values of the same words between two sentences to represent their idf similarity. The last three similarities are from WordNet.

For every feature, we can use it to get a sentence with the highest score. Then among these nine sentences chosen by nine features, we use voting method to choose the most repetitive sentence as the final linking result. When some sentences get the same votes, we choose the first one according to sentence order in the input news and comments.

3.2 Argument Label

Figure 2 shows the process for argument label.

Given a collection of sentences in the input file, we wish to discover topic distribution of every sentence through LDA model. We generate the input file for LDA first. For every sentence, we change it into its bag-of-words model representation, which assumes that the order of words can be neglected. During LDA modeling, we set the topic number to 15 according to the experiments. That is to say, later in K-means clustering, our feature is the 15-dimension vector. We run K-means to cluster all sentences into two categories. For every sentence pair, if the two sentences belong to the same category, then we set the label to in_favour, else, against.

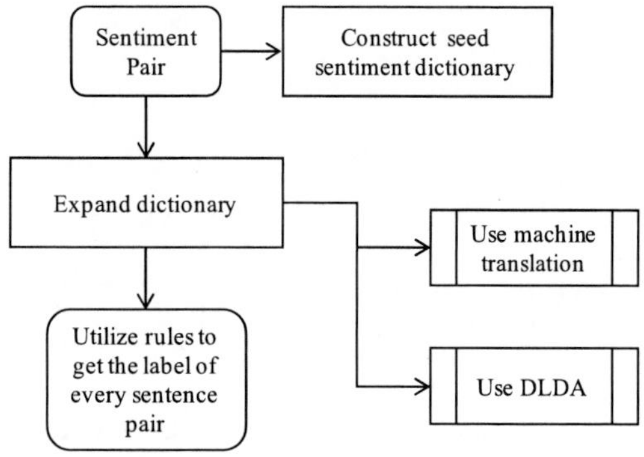

Figure 3: Sentiment label process

3.3 Sentiment Label

Figure 3 shows the process for sentiment label.

There are three kinds of seed sentiment dictionaries discovered from OpinionFinder system (MPQA, http://mpqa.cs.pitt.edu/). One is subjectivity lexicon, the other two are called Intensifier and Valenceshifters lexicon. Intensifier lexicon involves words which can improve the sentiment level. Valenceshifters lexicon involves words which can alter the sentiment label.

The original dictionary is in English. We use machine translation to add Italian vocabularies. With DLDA (Chen et al., 2014), we can get all sentiment weights of words in corpus. At last, the word which is not included in seed has the same polarity with a seed word if their sentiment weight distance can be ignored.

Through DLDA, every word gets a sentiment state. We map the sentiment state to a number of word score as in Table 1. We accumulate word score in a sentence to obtain the sentence score, which is then mapped to the sentiment label as in Table 2.

Sentiment state	Word score
Weak neg(only)	-1
Strong neg(only)	-2
Strong pos(only)	2
Weak pos(only)	1
Neutral	0
Intensifier+weak neg	-2
Intensifier+weak pos	2

Table 1: Scoring strategy

Note that when current sentence score is bigger than 0 and current word is in Valenceshifters and the score of current word is less than 0, sentence score = sentence score * (-1), or current sentence score is less than 0 and current word is in Valenceshifters and the score of current word is more than 0, sentence score strategy is the same. For any other conditions, we simply accumulate the word score.

Sentence final score	Label
>0	Positive
=0	Neutral
<0	Negative

Table 2: Mapping sentence score to sentiment label

4 Experiments

4.1 Content Linking

Threshold is used for extracting sentence. We choose the sentence as linking result only when the score (for Method 1) or the vote (for Method 2) is bigger than the threshold.

Thres hold	Linking Precision	Thres hold	Linking Precision
0	77.9	0.5	81.9
0.1	78.2	0.6	80.6
0.2	80.8	0.7	84.2
0.3	80.6	0.8	87.0
0.4	80.8	0.9	87.8

Table 3: The performance of Method 1

Table 3 and Table 4 show the performance of Method 1 and Method 2 in our experiments respectively. The first and third rows in Table 4 are the threshold. F1 to F9 refer to 9 features respectively (word vector, jaccard, idf, res, jcn, path, lexicon 2, lexicon 1 and lexicon 3) and the number means the vote for corresponding feature.

From Table 3, we can find out that, for Method 1, the bigger threshold usually can bring the higher precision. But the sentences we obtain may be fewer, too. This will cause low recall rate. According to the precision evaluation method used by MultiLing 2015, precision of 86 is high. Thus we can have good precision here. For Method 2 in Table 4, although its precision is a little lower than that of Method 1, it can also achieve good result. Lexicon 3 shows its good performance, other features like jaccard and idf perform well, too. Hence, how to combine them is important for us in the future. Besides, the linking precision of Italian is 10.1 with the threshold of 0.6 as shown in Table 5.

Threshold	**2**	**2**	**2**
F1	1	0	1
F2	1	1	1
F3	1	0	0
F4	1	0	0
F5	1	1	0
F6	1	0	0
F7	1	0	0
F8	1	0	0
F9	1	2	2
Linking Precision	**78.4**	**85.2**	**85.2**
Threshold	**3**	**3**	**3**
F1	1	1	1
F2	1	0	1
F3	1	0	1
F4	1	1	0
F5	1	0	0
F6	1	0	0
F7	1	0	1
F8	1	0	0
F9	1	2	2
Linking Precision	**78.2**	**82.7**	**82.6**

Table 4: The performance of Method 2

Thres hold	Linking Precision	Thres hold	Linking Precision
0.3	8.14	0.5	8.8
0.4	8.25	0.6	10.1

Table 5: The performance for Italian

4.2 Argument and Sentiment Label

From Table 6, we can find out that when we set the threshold at 0.2 and 0.3, we can get the highest precision in both argument label and sentiment label. However, unlike the linking precision mentioned above, the bigger thresholds result in lower precision. The reason may be that when we set a bigger threshold, the linking sentences we obtain are much fewer. Sometimes we can only get one or two sentence pairs. If there are any wrong answers in the results, it will obviously decrease the precision.

Thres hold	Argu ment	Senti ment	Thres hold	Argu ment	Senti ment
0	85.9	77.6	0.5	76.7	78.3
0.1	86.1	79.6	0.6	67.6	60.7
0.2	86.3	79.1	0.7	52.9	52.0
0.3	84.8	81.1	0.8	47.6	59.1
0.4	80.5	75.4	0.9	47.3	58.9

Table 6: The performance of Labeling

5 Conclusion

For content linking, our system has tried to mine both syntactic and semantic information, and the performances are good. For argument and sentiment labeling, we focus on machine learning algorithm and sentiment dictionaries. And there is still space for us to improve. Our future work is to find some better ways to mine and use more semantic features for both content linking and labeling.

Acknowledgments

This work was supported by the National Natural Science Foundation of China under Grant 91546121, 71231002 and 61202247; National Social Science Foundation of China under Grant 16ZDA055; EU FP7 IRSES MobileCloud Project 612212; the 111 Project of China under Grant B08004; Engineering Research Center of Information Networks, Ministry of Education; the project of Beijing Institute of Science and Technology Information; the project of CapInfo Company Limited.

References

Peeyush Aggarwal and Richa Sharma. 2016. Lexical and syntactic cues to identify reference scope of citance. In *BIRNDL@ JCDL*, pages 103–112.

Ahmet Aker, Fabio Celli, Adam Funk, Emina Kurtic, Mark Hepple, and Rob Gaizauskas. 2015. Sheffield-trento system for sentiment and argument structure enhanced comment-to-article linking in the online news domain.

David M Blei, Andrew Y Ng, and Michael I Jordan. 2003. Latent dirichlet allocation. *Journal of Machine Learning Research*, 3:993–1022.

Ziqiang Cao, Wenjie Li, and Dapeng Wu. 2016. Polyu at cl-scisumm 2016. In *BIRNDL@ JCDL*, pages 132–138.

Xue Chen, Wenqing Tang, Hao Xu, and Xiaofeng Hu. 2014. Double lda: A sentiment analysis model based on topic model. In *International Conference on Semantics, Knowledge and Grids*, pages 49–56.

J. A. Hartigan and M. A. Wong. 1979. Algorithm as 136: A k-means clustering algorithm. *Applied Statistics*, 28(1):100–108.

Alexandra Balahur Hristo Tanev. 2015. Tackling the onforums challenge.

Kokil Jaidka, Muthu Kumar Chandrasekaran, Sajal Rustagi, and Min-Yen Kan. 2016. Overview of the cl-scisumm 2016 shared task. In *BIRNDL@ JCDL*, pages 93–102.

Mijail Kabadjov, Josef Steinberger, Emma Barker, Udo Kruschwitz, and Massimo Poesio. 2015. Onforums: The shared task on online forum summarisation at multiling'15. In *Forum for Information Retrieval Evaluation*, pages 21–26.

Stefan Klampfl, Andi Rexha, and Roman Kern. 2016. Identifying referenced text in scientific publications by summarisation and classification techniques. In *BIRNDL@ JCDL*, pages 122–131.

Lei Li, Liyuan Mao, Yazhao Zhang, Junqi Chi, Taiwen Huang, Xiaoyue Cong, and Heng Peng. 2016. Cist system for cl-scisumm 2016 shared task. In *BIRNDL@ JCDL*, pages 156–167.

Kun Lu, Jin Mao, Gang Li, and Jian Xu. 2016. Recognizing reference spans and classifying their discourse facets. In *BIRNDL@ JCDL*, pages 139–145.

Bruno Malenfant and Guy Lapalme. 2016. Rali system description for cl-scisumm 2016 shared task. In *BIRNDL@ JCDL*, pages 146–155.

Diana Maynard and Adam Funk. 2011. Automatic detection of political opinions in tweets. In *Extended Semantic Web Conference*, pages 88–99. Springer.

Tomas Mikolov, Kai Chen, Greg Corrado, and Jeffrey Dean. 2013. Efficient estimation of word representations in vector space. *Computer Science*.

Luis Moraes, Shahryar Baki, Rakesh Verma, and Daniel Lee. 2016. University of houston at cl-scisumm 2016: Svms with tree kernels and sentence similarity. In *BIRNDL@ JCDL*, pages 113–121.

Tadashi Nomoto. 2016. Neal: A neurally enhanced approach to linking citation and reference. In *BIRNDL@ JCDL*, pages 168–174.

Horacio Saggion, Ahmed AbuRa'ed, and Francesco Ronzano. 2016. Trainable citation-enhanced summarization of scientific articles. In *BIRNDL@ JCDL*, pages 175–186.

Ultra-Concise Multi-genre Summarisation of Web2.0: towards Intelligent Content Generation

Elena Lloret, Ester Boldrini, Patricio Martínez-Barco, Manuel Palomar
Department of Software and Computing Systems
University of Alicante
Apdo. de correos, 99
E-03080 Alicante, Spain
{elloret,eboldrini,patricio,mpalomar}@dlsi.ua.es

Abstract

The electronic Word of Mouth has become the most powerful communication channel thanks to the wide usage of the Social Media. Our research proposes an approach towards the production of automatic ultra-concise summaries from multiple Web 2.0 sources. We exploit user-generated content from reviews and microblogs in different domains, and compile and analyse four types of ultra-concise summaries: a) positive information, b) negative information; c) both or d) objective information. The appropriateness and usefulness of our model is demonstrated by its successful results and great potential in real-life applications, thus meaning a relevant advancement of the state-of-the-art approaches.

1 Introduction and Motivation

The Web 2.0 has created a framework where users from all over the world express their opinion on a wide range of topics via different communication Social Media channels, such as blogs, fora, micro-blogs, reviews, etc. Undoubtedly, all this information is of great value in today's competitive business environment, increasing the need for businesses to collect, monitor, and analyse user-generated data on their own and on their competitors' Social Media, such as Twitter (He et al., 2015). Moreover, this context is also fostering the electronic Word of Mouth (eWOM) (Jansen et al., 2009), an unpaid form of promotion (Duan et al., 2008) in which customers share with other users their experience with the product they bought, for example. WOM is an ancient phenomenon originated in the streets orally, but now, with the flourishing of the Web 2.0 it has been evolved in eWOM, whose essence is the same; the only difference is that it is not implemented orally, but using the Social Media instead (Boldrini et al., 2010): fora, blogs, online reviews and microblogs. However, the huge amount and the heterogeneity of online data poses great challenges to the development of applications able to effectively retrieve, extract and synthesise the main content spread within Social Media. Due to the richness of Social Media data, its exploitation is being crucial for business-oriented applications, such as market analysis, competence monitoring or simply understanding the reasons behind customers' opinion on a product. Having at their disposal effective applications for information analysis and exploitation would mean for them having competitive advantage.

Recently, three Natural Language Processing (NLP) applications are gaining predominance, especially in the field of Social Media content analysis: i) information retrieval (Croft et al., 2009), ii) opinion mining (Pang and Lee, 2008) and iii) automatic text summarisation (Nenkova and McKeown, 2011). Information retrieval aims to search and determine relevant documents on the Web according to a specific user need or topic. The goal of opinion mining is to identify subjective language and classify it according to its sentiment or polarity (i.e., positive, negative or neutral information). Finally, text summarisation detects the most relevant pieces of information from one or multiple texts and presents the main ideas in a coherent fragment of text.

The main objective of this article is to apply the aforementioned NLP techniques to exploit the Social Media data generated through online reviews and microblogs. In particular, our aim is to produce innovative automatic ultra-concise summaries in the form of tweets (140 characters) reliable in terms of content (they reflect the opinions expressed on a topic positive/negative -) and form. Even if there are some previous studies on this topic (Ganesan et al., 2012), the novelty of our

Proceedings of the MultiLing 2017 Workshop on Summarization and Summary Evaluation Across Source Types and Genres, pages 37–46, Valencia, Spain, April 3, 2017. ©2017 Association for Computational Linguistics

approach comes from the usage of multiple textual genres simultaneously and the production of a ultra concise summary (multi-genre summarisation). This means that our final summary is presented to the user in the form of a Tweet. The summary is representative of what has been said on a predefined topic. It is reliable since we perform a robust treatment of our source data. We treat each of the sources separately (because each textual genre has specific needs) and then merge the distinctive and relevant information for automatically building up the tweet as final outcome.

Microblogs, and more especially tweets, have a direct impact on eWOM communication. They empower people to share these brand-affecting points of view anywhere to almost anyone. Moreover, Princeton Survey Research Associates International[1] found that the microblogging site Twitter experienced massive amounts of growth over the past years with millions of new users joining and engaging with the site on a daily basis (Smith and Brennen, 2012). While the conciseness of microblogs keeps people from writing extensive reflections, it is exactly the micro part that makes microblogs peculiar if compared with other eWOM channels, such as blogs, webs, etc. Moreover, the advantage of having a tweet as a final outcome is that: a) we provide immediate information, b) users can take it and exploit it in the way they prefer (i.e. post it) and c) have a complete overview, comprehensive of different genres content in a friendly format, and d) save a lot of their time since the system carries out the job for them: retrieving, analysing, selecting, and providing them with the information they are looking for. Due to the limited length of a tweet, it is necessary to analyse to what extent and how current approaches could be adapted.

The motivation of our article lies on the fact that microblog is one the most used Social Media channel and thus considered as a point of reference for many users. This implies that the generation we do of brief summaries would be useful for users that can use it directly in their Social Networks. Microblogs have the potential of reaching a huge number of users. But not only normal users can take advantage of it; for instance a company can exploit such ultra-concise summaries disseminating them through different channels for advertising purposes, to attract more customers or to make its potential customers aware of the high reputation of their products; thus, making this technology a real-life application that will allow users to save a lot of time and effort since the system will do the job automatically analysing the texts selected and summarising their content in a reliable way.

The paper is organised as follows: Section 2 presents the most relevant related work, while Section 3 the corpus creation and Section 4 its annotation. Section 5 describes the methodology for generating ultra-concise summaries and Section 6 the evaluation of the results obtained. Section 7 analyses our approach in-depth, and finally, Section 8 outlines the main conclusions and future work.

2 Related Work

In the last years, there has been much interest in summarisation from Social Media, within the wider context of opinion summarisation. Twitter is now the most popular microblogging service. It is a huge repository of data and it is gaining popularity in different NLP tasks, especially in automatic text summarisation focusing on generating brief summaries starting from a collection of texts like microblog entries, like Tweets (O'Connor et al., 2010; Sharifi et al., 2010; Kim et al., 2014) or enriched with other sources of information, like Webpage links or newswire (Liu et al., 2011). In (Sharifi et al., 2010) a trending topic is considered as a starting point from which all related posts are collected and summarised. They generally use machine learning algorithms to detect the sentences mostly related to the topic phrase. In (Inouye and Kalita, 2011) a comparative analysis of different summarisation techniques is carried out to determine which is the most adequate for this type of summaries, and it is concluded that simple word frequency and redundancy reduction are the best techniques for the Twitter topics summarisation. In (Weng et al., 2011), the approach to summarise Twitter posts consists of two stages: i) classification of the posts and responses in different groups, according to their intention (interrogation, sharing, discussion and chat) and ii) analysis of different strategies for building the summary through sentiment analysis techniques or simply analysing the responses for each post. Their final summaries are generated depending on the category they belong (e.g., if the summarised posts are within the sharing groups, the summary is a pie

[1] http://www.psrai.com/ (last access 30 January 2017)

Domain	Technology	Motor
Topic	Mobile phones	Cars
Number of topics	10	10
Number of tweets per topic	13	10
Number of online reviews per topic	9	10
Microblogs (Avg. Number of words per tweet)	28.05	14.76
Microblogs (Number of words in total)	3647	1476
Reviews (Avg. Number of words per review)	146.30	156.13
Reviews (Number of words in total)	13167	15613

Table 1: Corpus statistics.

chart showing the percentage of positive and negative opinions). Other relevant studies aim at generating other types of summaries, like event summaries (Chakrabarti and Punera, 2011) or ultra-concise opinion summaries (Ganesan et al., 2012). In the former, the goal is to produce a real-time summary of events, focusing on the American Football games, and analysing the performance of different summarisers. In the latter, the objective is to generate a tweet from a set of reviews, where each tweet is a summary of a key opinion in text, and it relies on techniques based on Web N-grams.

Our research idea is based on (Ganesan et al., 2012), but the main novelty and added value of our research with respect to it is precisely the multi-genre perspective addressed: starting simultaneously from multiple sources of information, tweets and online reviews we treat them and produce an ultra concise summary that is reliable and representative in terms of content. This output can be directly used by the user in his own Social Networks and not to waste their time in analysing what they found and prepare a summary of the huge amount of information available.

3 Corpus Creation

We automatically gathered a corpus of online reviews and tweets in English for 10 different mobile phones and 10 cars using the crawler developed in (Fernández et al., 2010). A crawler is an automatic process in charge of retrieving and extracting the HTML content of a Website. In this process, relevant information sources are identified (e.g. Websites of reviews), and then the content of useful web pages within the selected sources of information are retrieved, downloaded, and extracted in an automatic, quick and easy manner using the well-known vector space model. This manner, a corpus with a large number of documents can be created automatically. Using this crawler, 10 mobile phone brands and 10 car brand models were selected to conduct the experiments. For each brand, we obtained on average 10 microblogs extracted from Twitter and 10 online reviews from Amazon[2] and WhatCar[3], having in total 400 texts. We selected cars and mobile phones, since they are frequently discussed by people with different profiles and at the same time they are from two different domains (important for demonstrating the efficiency of our approach in multi-domain contexts). Furthermore, mobile phones and car topics can be seen as in between the high-level terminology complexity of a specific and technical domain such as medicine for example and an easier one like food or music. In our case, for this step of our research we focused on a medium level complexity topic to check if our techniques were pertinent for a real-life application.

Table 1 summarises the main features of our corpus. Analysing the specific properties and features for each of the Social Media textual genres, the most outstanding difference is the length of the texts. While the tweets are very short, having no more than 28 words on average, the reviews are quite longer, with more than 145 words on average. Both textual genres will be therefore complementary, tweets providing conciseness, whereas reviews providing opinions in a specific context.

4 Annotation Process

Once the documents were retrieved, we pre-processed them by extracting only the main text; a very important step since we eliminate all pos-

[2]http://www.amazon.com (last access 30 January 2017)
[3]http://www.whatcar.com (last access 30 January 2017)

sible characters that are not part of the information, links, and emoticons. Then, we started the annotation process, where one expert annotator manually labelled the documents using the coarse-grained version of the EmotiBlog annotation schema (Boldrini et al., 2010). To have the documents annotated by just one expert was considered enough for this preliminary study, since the EmotiBlog model had been previously evaluated (Boldrini, 2012) and proved to be easy to use. The annotation schema developed in EmotiBlog was created for automatic systems to detect the subjective expressions in the new textual genres of the Web 2.0 and has been employed to improve the performance of different NLP applications dealing with complex tasks, including opinion summarisation, where it obtained satisfactory results (Balahur et al., 2009).

Although EmotiBlog was originally a very fine-grained annotation scheme, we decided to use the less grained part of the resource, since our research purposes at this level only required to detect subjectivity and classify the polarity of a statement. Therefore, the expert annotator labelled the corpus at sentence level during 4 weeks in part time dedication using the following EmotiBlog elements: POLARITY (positive/negative/neutral) + INTENSITY (high/medium/low). The fragment below shows an example of labelled sentence for the topic "Nokia 2700", a subjective sentence whose polarity is positive, with a high intensity.

```
<phenomenon degree1="high"
category="phrase"
polarity="positive"
source="w" target="Nokia
2700" confidence="high">It's
inexpensive, it's primarily a
phone but it has some useful
features, it's neat and it works
well.</phenomenon>
```

We selected the abovementioned elements of the EmotiBlog model since our purpose is to discriminate sentences between objective/subjective and from the subjective ones discriminate them into positive/negative and finally the summarisation system will treat those two groups to produce a reliable ultra-concise summary that reflects the reality of users feelings. This process implies the added challenge for the summarisation system to be able to treat the two typologies (objective/subjective), quite challenging task if we take into consideration the high language variability present in the Web 2.0 (Pacea, 2011). The reason why we performed manual annotation was because we wanted to ensure a precise labelling and minimise cascade errors derived from the use of NLP tools. This manner we can focus more on the evaluation of the automatic summarisation approach.

5 Ultra-concise Summary Generation

To the best of our knowledge, this is one of the first attempts aiming at generating this new type of summaries starting from text sources of different nature (i.e., multi-genre), and about different opinion polarities (positive/negative/objective). This requires that the summarisation system has high coverage to produce such a small text with full meaning, relevant to the topic, and with grammatical adequacy. These types of summaries have enormous benefits as presented in Section 1. As it was previously said, the ultra-concise summarisation generation approach employed in this research is novel considering the following main aspects. First of all, it is able to deal with different types of Web 2.0 textual genres (tweets and reviews) thus employing NLP techniques able to treat the linguistic phenomena encountered (thanks to the annotation performed beforehand). The proposed approach takes as a starting point the corpus previously created, and then it performs a series of steps to determine the relevant information, and analysing the most appropriate manner to present it in the form of a tweet. In addition its modular architecture allows the inclusion of tools for deeper language/linguistic/content analysis. Figure 1 depicts an overview of our proposed approach. Next, the stages involved in the process are explained in more detail:

1. **Polarity detection and classification:** our main goal in this stage is to group the sentences into three sets: one for the positive, one for the negatives, and one for the objectives. In this manner, taking as a starting point a set of topic-related reviews and tweets, the first stage is to detect and classify the opinions contained. In our research work, we take advantage of the manual annotation process previously explained, because this manner, precise information concerning the positive, negative and objective sentences is obtained.

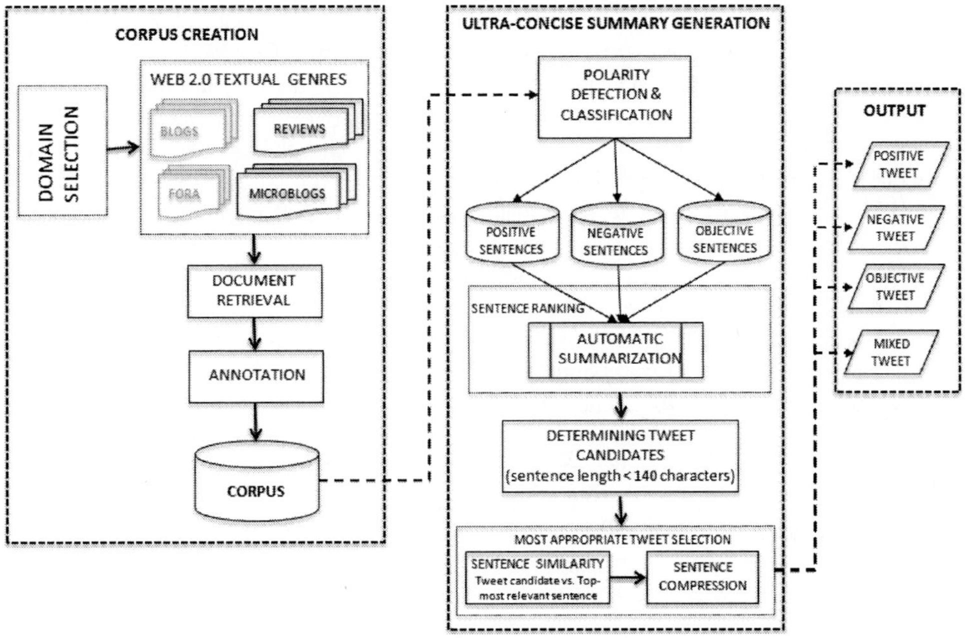

Figure 1: Overview of our proposed approach.

2. **Sentence ranking:** the aim of this stage is to assign a relevance score to each positive, negative or objective sentence. This relevance score is determined automatically, relying on automatic summarisation techniques. Specifically, two heuristics were used to compute the relevance for a sentence: term frequency and noun-phrase length. On the one hand, term frequency is a statistical technique that assumes that the more important sentences are determined by the most frequent words, without taking into account the words that do not carry any semantic information (i.e., stopwords such as "the", "a", etc.). On the other hand, the use of noun-phrase length has a linguistic motivation (Givón, 1990), where it is stated that longer noun-phrases carry more important information. Then, for calculating the score of each sentence, these two heuristics were combined, thus considering more important those sentences containing longer noun-phrases composed of high frequent words. The combination of both techniques has been proven to work fine for producing automatic summaries by means of COMPENDIUM summariser (Lloret and Palomar, 2013).

3. **Determining candidate text fragments for tweets:** although a relevance score was assigned to each sentence, one of the key issues of the task we are facing is how to produce tweet informative enough, ensuring at the same time, the 140 characters length restriction. At this stage, regardless of the relevance for each sentence, we identify from each group of sentences those ones not exceeding the 140 characters length to be combined with the relevance score in the next stage. Although this may seem a trivial approach, the current semantic analysis and natural language generation tools are not capable of dealing with the textual genres of the Web 2.0, making a lot of errors that could be detrimental for the final summaries.

4. **Selecting the most appropriate tweet:** having on the one hand, the score for each sentences, and on the other hand, the group of sentences that would fit the tweet length, an added value of our proposed approach is to take into account in a joint manner the relevance sentence score, distinguishing them with respect to their polarity, and the potential tweet candidates that fit with the right length. The strategy followed in this stage is to select as tweets the ones that are most

similar to the top-most relevant sentence in each group, but at the same time, not surpassing 140 characters. For achieving this we used the cosine similarity measure, where the tweet candidate whose cosine score is most similar to the sentences that have been identified are more relevant is extracted as final tweet. This works fine for the generation of positive, negative or objective tweets. However, when a mixed tweet needs to be produced, the result of combining subjective and objective information may be ending with a sentence longer than 140 characters. If this happens, we use the same method as in (Lloret et al., 2013) for compressing sentences. In the end, we obtain four tweets (positive, negative, objective, and one containing a mix of subjective/objective information). We therefore propose these four tweets as reliable ultra-concise summaries.

All these stages together with the corpus creation are then included in a semi-automatic sequential process, where basic and intermediate NLP components are used in order to analyse and pre-process the input documents to the summarisation engine.

6 Evaluation and Results

The evaluation of our ultra-concise summarisation approach was carried out by two expert users who evaluated in an independent manner the automatic ultra-concise summaries (i.e. the generated tweets). For performing this evaluation, we relied on the qualitative criteria employed in the TAC conferences[4]. These criteria were: a) the content of the summary, b) its readability and c) its overall responsiveness. The first criterion determines whether the tweet reflects important information of the source inputs; the second assesses whether the tweet is well-written and easy to understand; and the third evaluates if it is reliable and suitable for a real-life application. Evaluating our results with these criteria allows us determining if the product we reach is useful because it is of a high quality, so that no additional treatment is needed. They were evaluated from a conceptual point of view and the general idea expressed, rather than from the individual words building up the summaries.

[4]http://www.nist.gov/tac/ (last access 30 January 2017)

For each topic (mobile phone and cars) we produce different alternatives as tweets: i) positive information; ii) negative information; iii) objective information; and iv) mixing subjective and objective information. Each of these tweets (40 in total) was rated according to a 3-level Likert scale, with values ranging from 1 to 3 (1=poor or very poor; 2=barely acceptable; and 3=good or very good). The reason for choosing such scale and not a 5-level one was to avoid assessment dispersion. In our case, the agreement between the two assessors was quite high: 60% for content, 75% for readability, and 65% for overall responsiveness criteria, meaning that they both agree in the score assigned to the summary. It is important to stress that the assessors had access to the original reviews and tweets, from which the automatic tweets were generated, and they read them in advance for being able to determine whether the automatic tweets were reliable and a good representative of the source documents. Table 2 shows the average results obtained for each type of automatically generated tweet. Last two columns provide the global average obtained taking into account all the results.

The results are very encouraging, meaning that our proposed approach can be considered as appropriate for synthesising in one tweet or ultra-concise summary relevant information. Next, we show an example of a potential mixed Tweet with 126 characters that contains subjective and objective information that belong to the group that has obtained the best results:

"Most annoyingly, the alarm is MUCH too quiet. Aside from the alarm though, this is a fab little phone which I highly recommend."

Generally, the results for each criterion are high, since they are over 2.50, and in most of the cases, very close to 3, the maximum value. Thus, tweets are readable, easy to understand, and reflect relevant information or the key aspects of the phones. If we have a look at the results obtained, we can also notice a better performance in the case of negative sentences. This could be due to the fact that generally negative concepts are expressed in a much more strong and direct way than positive ones, thus are easier to detect and treat from a linguistic point of view. Moreover, we can also appreciate that the objective sentences have lower

	Content		Readability		Over. Resp.		Global	
	Phones	**Cars**	**Phones**	**Cars**	**Phones**	**Cars**	**Phones**	**Cars**
Positive	2.55	**2.70**	2.65	2.65	2.55	2.70	2.58	2.68
Negative	2.72	2.50	2.83	2.60	2.76	2.65	2.76	2.58
Objective	2.01	2.35	2.61	2.40	2.22	2.35	2.22	2.37
Mixed	**2.75**	**2.70**	**2.85**	**2.80**	**2.77**	**2.75**	**2.77**	**2.75**

Table 2: Average results for the ultra-concise summaries generated with our approach

	Content		Readab.ility		Over. Resp.		Global	
	Phones	**Cars**	**Phones**	**Cars**	**Phones**	**Cars**	**Phones**	**Cars**
Our approach	**2.75**	**2.70**	**2.85**	**2.80**	**2.77**	**2.75**	**2.77**	**2.75**
Swotti	2.22	2.35	2.45	2.50	2.30	2.40	2.32	2.42
Ganesan	1.20	1.30	1.45	1.85	1.25	1.45	1.30	1.48
COMPENDIUMsem	1.75	2.65	1.65	2.75	1.70	2.60	1.70	2.67

Table 3: Comparison results for mixed tweet generation across systems

performance and after having analysed our test set, we reach the conclusion that this is because of the huge amount of advertisement that companies launch in such communication channels, adding noise and influencing in a negative way the retrieval of the sentences and thus the performance of the system. Analysing more in detail the generated tweets, we find some beneficial aspects of our approach and some other aspects with room for improvement. Concerning the positive ones, the modularity of our approach makes it easy to adapt it to other textual genres and languages. Moreover, a strong advantage of our approach is that it is able to produce different types of tweets to be used for different purposes. Each type of tweet can be more or less suitable depending on the users' needs and interests, thus allowing taking into account the user/company's profile. For instance, if a company wants to emphasise a good feature of a product, a positive tweet entry would be the best. In contrast, if they want to improve the weaknesses of their products, a negative tweet could be more appropriate (always seeing this automatic generated tweet as an additional tool to be properly managed by market experts). On the other hand, we also observed some cases in which the automatic tweets generated did not meet our expectations. We found that some original tweets were in other languages than English, such as Spanish or French, and therefore they were counted as incorrect, since we are focusing only in the English language. This was probably due to the fact that the crawler used did not filter the language of the tweets, because this did not occur for the reviews. However, this stresses the necessity and importance of multilingual approaches that could deal with these challenges and exploit a larger amount of data. Another issue that is worth discussing is the informality, frequently employed in Web 2.0 content. In our case, this was higher in tweets than in on-line reviews, and although, the automatic tweets were not much affected for this, this could be a problematic issue when dealing with highly informal texts.

For both domains tested, the mixed summaries were the ones with best results. To compare our summaries in the form of a tweet with respect to other existing approaches, we took into account the following systems, and we evaluated the results following the same criteria as for the previous evaluation of our approach:

- COMPENDIUMsem (Vodolazova et al., 2012) for determining relevant sentences. This summariser takes into account semantic features, such as concept identification and disambiguation, textual entailment and anaphora resolution.

- The approach proposed in (Ganesan et al., 2012), which is able to produce ultra-concise opinion summaries as well.

- Swotti[5], which is a commercial system that provides summarised opinion information for

[5]http://swotti.starmedia.com/ (last access 30 January 2017)

a wide range of products.

Table 3 shows the comparison results of our approach (mixed tweet configuration) with respect to the other systems, where the last two columns provide the global average per row. As it can be seen, our approach obtains the best performance, showing again its appropriateness to be used in real-life applications. From the comparison results, we would like to note that even if we also tested summarisation approaches relying on semantic knowledge the results of these summaries were lower than when using simple word frequency techniques, as in our approach. This confirms the findings in (Inouye and Kalita, 2011), and verifies the power of lexical-based techniques for summarisation. This could be also seen as a competitive method for the generation of ultra-concise summaries. In addition, the results achieved with Swotti, a real on-line platform that provides opinion summarisation, could not surpass the ones obtained with our approach either.

7 Potentials and Limitations of Our Approach

After having described our approach and the results obtained it is worth underlying that, since this the first step of an experimental approach, we decided to take into account only the text. As explained above, all non-conventional characters were deleted. In addition, emoticons have also been removed, however our idea is to take them into account for next steps, since they are usually charged with polarity that could also be an added value for the correct text interpretation.

The retrieval and pre processing stages confirmed the fact that the text available in the Social Media is extremely informal and it does not always follow the conventional rules. Many are the cases of informal languages that contain sayings or collocations hard to interpret automatically. They will be taken into account in future work, since the EmotiBlog annotation model is able to capture and interpret them in terms of polarity. In addition to semantic challenges, the issue of informality is a main concern. Last but not least, the fact of working with different textual genres poses the problem of having to deal with different linguistic phenomena, typical in one or other genre. The result of this is that, despite the satisfactory performance we also obtained cases with room for improvement. Example of this are:

- *Help please?!*
- *2.5mm Standard Headset Adapter for LG GW520 [Wireless Phone Accessory]: A top quality standard headset adapter (... http://amzn.to/wnzLVP*
- *Easy AdSense Pro by Unreal Here is download link LG KS360/ KS365 PC suite/Sync/USB Driver for http://goo.gl/fb/uxV5o*

From the examples above, we can deduce that in the cases in which the system performance was not satisfactory, we obtain sentences with no relevant content in most of the cases. In all the cases in which the system performance was satisfactory, examples of sentences are the following ones:

- *The only annoying thing I do find is all the Blackberry apps are geared up for the USA, not UK, which limits their desirability.*
- *The battery life is good and will last me 2-3 days if I am careful.*
- *All the Blackberry apps are geared up for the USA. The internet drains is pretty quickly. The battery is good and will last me 2-3 days.*

As it can be seen, the content is relevant to the topic search. In addition to this, in the third case we obtain a mixed tweet, which includes different ideas taken from the positive, negative and objective sentences. This is very important to maintain the relevance of the content and thus the quality and reliability of the system output.

8 Conclusion and Future Work

In this article, we presented an innovative method for creating an effective system that produces ultra-concise summaries with no more that 140 characters (i.e., in the form of a tweet). The approach represents an advancement of the state-of-the-art approach since we work with multiple textual genres simultaneously and produce a reliable ultra concise summary. We start from the information contained in a selected corpus composed of on-line reviews and microblogs written in English about "mobile phones and cars" and more concretely we selected a set of 10 cell phones and 10 cars of different brands. We presented our corpus and the annotation process carried out. For the corpus annotation, we applied the coarse grained version of the EmotiBlog annotation schema that is a fine-grained annotation schema for the detection of the subjectivity in the new textual genres of the Web 2.0. We took advantage of such annotation to propose a novel summarisation approach that employed statistical and linguistic techniques for detecting relevant sentences. We generated four types of ultra-concise summaries (or tweets) that were then evaluated following a standard qualitative framework, and compared to similar approaches. From the results obtained we conclude that our approach is reliable and appropriate for generating this types of summaries. The successful performance of the tweets (in terms of content reliability and syntactic adequacy) clearly indicates that they can be used within a real-life application. The selection of which tweet to show is out of the scope of this paper, and this would depend on the target users and purpose of the tweet. However, one strategy that could be adopted would be to rely on existing automatic rating models, such as EmotiReview (Boldrini et al., 2011). This manner depending on the rating given to a specific product, we could decide which type of tweet should be generated.

Despite the good results achieved, there are several issues that have to be tackled for improving the generation of ultra-concise summaries and that we plan to tackle as future work. On the one hand, in the short-term, we will mainly focus on two aspects: the multilinguality and the inclusion of more Web 2.0 textual genres and domains. This manner, we will be able to extend our approach to languages, such as Italian or Spanish, as well as to deal with other type of texts, such as fora, or blogs and increase the domains such as tourism, politics, etc. Moreover, we want to analyse in more detail the impact of each proposed stage in the summarisation process, as well as the influence of each textual genre. In this manner, we will substitute the manual annotation for sentiment analysis for an automatic one as well as we will analyse more features for sentiment analysis (e.g. target, intensity, etc.), and we will test other summarisation techniques. On the other hand, for the medium and long-term research, we will increase the size of the annotated corpus, and we will use it to train a machine learning system that automatically detects and classifies the objective/subjective information. In addition, a topic detection stage able to identify concepts and their relationships would be necessary in order to personalise the resulting summaries. Other important issues to take into account will be the informality of the text and some sentiment-analysis-related phenomena, such as irony, that were out of the scope of the paper, due to its great difficulty. The informality of a text could be detected and used to normalize the texts using for instance the TENOR tool (Mosquera and Moreda, 2012), or vice versa, to produce an informal summary in the form of a tweet. For detecting ironic expressions, we could also rely on already existing approaches, such as the one described in (Reyes et al., 2012).

Acknowledgments

This research work has been partially funded by the Generalitat Valenciana and the Spanish Government through the projects DIIM2.0 (PROMETEOII/2014/001), TIN2015-65100-R and TIN2015-65136-C2-2-R.

References

Alexandra Balahur, Elena Lloret, Ester Boldrini, Andrés Montoyo, Manuel Palomar, and Patricio Martínez-Barco. 2009. Summarizing threads in blogs using opinion polarity. In *Proceedings of the Workshop on Events in Emerging Text Types*, pages 23–31, Borovets, Bulgaria, September. Association for Computational Linguistics.

Ester Boldrini, Alexandra Balahur, Patricio Martínez-Barco, and Andrés Montoyo. 2010. Emotiblog: A finer-grained and more precise learning of subjectivity expression models. In *Proceedings of the Fourth Linguistic Annotation Workshop*, pages 1–10, Uppsala, Sweden, July. Association for Computational Linguistics.

Ester Boldrini, Javier Fernández, José Manuel Gómez, and Patricio Martínez-Barco. 2011. Emotiblog: Towards a finer-grained sentiment analysis and its application to opinion mining. In *Proceedings of IV Jornadas TIMM*, pages 49–54.

Ester Boldrini. 2012. *EmotiBlog: A Model to Learn Subjective Information Detection in the New Textual Genres of the Web 2.0 -a Multilingual and Multi-Genre Approach.* Ph.D. thesis, University of Alicante.

Deepayan Chakrabarti and Kunal Punera. 2011. Event summarization using tweets. In *Proceedings of the Fifth International Conference on Weblogs and Social Media, Barcelona, Catalonia, Spain, July 17-21, 2011.*

Bruce Croft, Donald Metzler, and Trevor Strohman. 2009. *Search Engines: Information Retrieval in Practice.* Addison-Wesley Publishing Company, USA, 1st edition.

Wenjing Duan, Bin Gu, and Andrew B. Whinston. 2008. Do Online Reviews Matter? - An Empirical Investigation of Panel Data. *Decision Support Systems*, 45(4):1007–1016, November.

Javi Fernández, José Manuel Gómez, and Patricio Martínez Barco. 2010. Evaluation of web information retrieval systems on restricted domains. *Procesamiento del Lenguaje Natural*, 45:273–276.

Kavita Ganesan, ChengXiang Zhai, and Evelyne Viegas. 2012. Micropinion generation: An unsupervised approach to generating ultra-concise summaries of opinions. In *Proceedings of the 21st International Conference on World Wide Web*, pages 869–878, New York, NY, USA. ACM.

Talmy Givón. 1990. *Syntax: A functional-typological introduction. Volume II. Amsterdam: John Benjamins. XXV, 553 pages. (Volume 1: 1984 (XX, 464 pages).*

Wu He, Harris Wu, Gongjun Yan, Vasudeva Akula, and Jiancheng Shen. 2015. A novel social media competitive analytics framework with sentiment benchmarks. *Information & Management*, 52(7):801–812.

David Inouye and Jugal K. Kalita. 2011. Comparing twitter summarization algorithms for multiple post summaries. In *PASSAT/SocialCom 2011, Privacy, Security, Risk and Trust (PASSAT), 2011 IEEE Third International Conference on and 2011 IEEE Third International Conference on Social Computing (SocialCom), Boston, MA, USA, 9-11 Oct., 2011*, pages 298–306.

B.J. Jansen, M. Zhang, K. Sobel, and A. Chowdury. 2009. Twitter power: Tweets as electronic word of mouth. *Journal of American Society of Information Science*, 60(11):2169–2188, November.

Tae-Yeon Kim, Jaekwang Kim, Jaedong Lee, and Jee-Hyong Lee. 2014. A tweet summarization method based on a keyword graph. In *Proceedings of the 8th International Conference on Ubiquitous Information Management and Communication*, ICUIMC '14, pages 96:1–96:8, New York, NY, USA. ACM.

Fei Liu, Yang Liu, and Fuliang Weng. 2011. Why is "sxsw" trending?: Exploring multiple text sources for twitter topic summarization. In *Proceedings of the Workshop on Languages in Social Media*, LSM '11, pages 66–75, Stroudsburg, PA, USA. Association for Computational Linguistics.

Elena Lloret and Manuel Palomar. 2013. COMPENDIUM: a text summarisation tool for generating summaries of multiple purposes, domains, and genres. *Natural Language Engineering*, 19:147–186, 4.

Elena Lloret, María Teresa Romá-Ferri, and Manuel Palomar. 2013. COMPENDIUM: A text summarization system for generating abstracts of research papers. *Data & Knowledge Engineering*, 88:164–175.

Alejandro Mosquera and Paloma Moreda. 2012. Tenor: A lexical normalisation tool for spanish web 2.0 texts. In Petr Sojka, Ales Hork, Ivan Kopecek, and Karel Pala, editors, *Text, Speech and Dialogue - 15th International Conference, TSD 2012, Brno, Czech Republic, September 3-7, 2012. Proceedings*, volume 7499 of *Lecture Notes in Computer Science*, pages 535–542. Springer.

Ani Nenkova and Kathleen McKeown. 2011. Automatic summarization. *Foundations and Trends in Information Retrieval*, 5(2-3):103–233.

Brendan O'Connor, Michel Krieger, and David Ahn. 2010. Tweetmotif: Exploratory search and topic summarization for twitter. In *Proceedings of the Fourth International Conference on Weblogs and Social Media, ICWSM 2010, Washington, DC, USA, May 23-26, 2010.*

O. Pacea. 2011. CorpTweet: Brands, Language and Identity in Web 2.0. *SERIA FILOLOGIE*, 22(2):157–168.

Bo Pang and Lillian Lee. 2008. Opinion mining and sentiment analysis. *Foundations and Trends in Information Retrieval:*, 2(1-2):1–135, January.

Antonio Reyes, Paolo Rosso, and Davide Buscaldi. 2012. From Humor Recognition to Irony Detection: The Figurative Language of Social Media. *Data & Knowledge Engineering*, 74:1–12.

Beaux Sharifi, Mark-Anthony Hutton, and Jugal Kalita. 2010. Summarizing microblogs automatically. In *Human Language Technologies: The 2010 Annual Conference of the North American Chapter of the Association for Computational Linguistics*, pages 685–688, Los Angeles, California, June. Association for Computational Linguistics.

A. Smith and J. Brennen. 2012. Twitter use 2012. technical report. Technical report.

Tatiana Vodolazova, Elena Lloret, Rafael Muñoz, and Manuel Palomar. 2012. A comparative study of the impact of statistical and semantic features in the framework of extractive text summarization. In *Proceedings of the 15th International Conference on Text, Speech, and Dialogue Conference*, TSD '12, pages 306–313.

Jui-Yu Weng, Cheng-Lun Yang, Bo-Nian Chen, Yen-Kai Wang, and Shou-De Lin. 2011. IMASS: An intelligent microblog analysis and summarization system. In *Proceedings of the ACL-HLT 2011 System Demonstrations*, pages 133–138, Portland, Oregon, June. Association for Computational Linguistics.

Machine Learning Approach to Evaluate MultiLingual Summaries

Samira Ellouze and **Maher Jaoua** and **Lamia Hadrich Belguith**
ANLP-RG, MIRACL Laboratory, FSEG Sfax, University of Sfax, Sfax, Tunisia
Samira.Ellouze@fsegs.rnu.tn, maher.jaoua@fsegs.rnu.tn, l.belguith@fsegs.rnu.tn

Abstract

The present paper introduces a new MultiLing text summary evaluation method. This method relies on machine learning approach which operates by combining multiple features to build models that predict the human score (overall responsiveness) of a new summary. We have tried several single and "ensemble learning" classiers to build the best model. We have experimented our method in summary level evaluation where we evaluate the quality of each text summary separately. The correlation between built models and human score is better than the correlation between the baselines and the manual score.

1 Introduction

Nowadays, the evaluation of summarization systems is an important step in the development cycle of those systems. In fact, it accelerates the cycle of development by giving an analysis of errors, making an optimization of systems and comparing each system with others. The evaluation of text summary covers its content, its linguistic quality or both. Whatever the type of evaluation (content and/or linguistic quality), the evaluation of system summary output is a difficult task given that in most times there is not a single good summary. In the extreme case, two summaries of the same documents set may have completely different words and/or sentences with different structures. Several metrics have been evaluated the content, the linguistic quality and the overall responsiveness of MonoLing text summaries. We can cite ROUGE (Lin and Hovy, 2003), BE (Hovy et al., 2006), AutoSummENG (Giannakopoulos et al., 2008), BEwTE (Tratz and Hovy, 2008) , etc. Some of those metircs can assess MultiLing text summaries such as ROUGE and AutoSummENG. But, those features can only evaluate the content of MultiLing text summaries.

To encourage research to develop automatic multilingual multi-documents summarization systems a new task, dubbed MultiLing Pilot (Giannakopoulos et al., 2011), has been introduced for the first time in TAC2011 conference. Later, the two workshops 2013 ACL MultiLing Pilot (Giannakopoulos, 2013) and MultiLing 2015 at SIGdial 2015 (Giannakopoulos et al., 2015) have been organised with the same purpose as MultiLing Pilot 2011. The participated summarization systems in the MultiLing task have been assessed using automatic content metrics such as ROUGE-1, ROUGE-2 and MeMoG and a manual metric named Overall Respensiveness which covers the content and the linguistic quality of a text summary. However, the manual evaluation of both the content and the linguistic quality of multilingual multi-documents summarization systems is an arduous and costly process. In addition, the automatic evaluation of only the content of summary is not enough because a summary should also have a good linguistic quality. For this reason, automatic metrics that evaluate the content and the linguistic quality of summaries from several languages should be developed. In this context, we propose a new method based on a machine learning approach for evaluating the overall quality of automatic text summaries. This method could predict the human score (Overall Reponsiveness) of English and Arabic text summaries by combining multiple content and linguistic quality features.

The rest of the paper is organized in the following way: First in Section 2 we introduce the main metrics that have been proposed to evaluate text summaries; then in Section 3 we explain the methodology adopted in our work. In Section 4 we present the different experiments and results

Proceedings of the MultiLing 2017 Workshop on Summarization and Summary Evaluation Across Source Types and Genres, pages 47–54,
Valencia, Spain, April 3, 2017. ©2017 Association for Computational Linguistics

for summary level evaluation. Finally, Section 5 describes the main conclusions and possible future works.

2 Related Works

The summary evaluation task started as Monoling evaluation task. Several manual and automatic metrics have been developed to evaluate the content and the linguistic quality of text summary. Manual evaluation is expensive and time-consuming. Then, there is a need to assess text summaries automatically. One of the standards in automatic evaluation is ROUGE (Lin and Hovy, 2003). It measures overlapping content between a candidate summary and reference summaries. ROUGE metric scores are obtained through the comparison of common words: N-grams. Later, Giannakopoulos et al. (2008) introduced AutoSummENG metric, which is based on statistical extracting of textual information from the summary. The information extracted from the summary, represents a set of relations between n-grams in this summary. The n-grams and the relations are represented as a graph where the nodes are the N-grams and the edges represent the relations between them. The calculation of the similarity is performed by comparing the graph of the candidate summary with the graph of each reference summary. In a subsequent work, (Giannakopoulos and Karkaletsis, 2010) have presented Merge Model Graph (MeMoG) which is another variation of AutoSummENG based on n-gram graphs. This variation calculates the merged graph of all reference summaries. Then, it compares the candidate summary graph to the merged graph of reference summaries. Afterwards, the SIMetrix (Summary Input similarity Metrics) measurement was developed by (Louis and Nenkova, 2013); it assesses a candidate summary by comparing it with the source documents. The SIMetrix computes ten measures of similarity based on the comparison between the source documents and the candidate summary. Among the used similarity measures we cite the cosine similarity, the divergence of Jensen-Shannon, the divergence of Kullback-Leibler, etc.

Recently, (Giannakopoulos and Karkaletsis, 2013) proposed NPowER (N-gram graph Powered Evaluation via Regression) metric, which presents a combination of AutoSummENG and MeMoG. They build a linear regression model that predicts a manual (human) score. All the above metrics (ROUGE, AutoSummENG, NPowER and SIMetrix) are used in monolingual and multilingual summary evaluation. Same of those metrics are adapted to multilingual evaluation while others (i.e. AutoSummENG) can from the beginning, support multilingual evaluation.

3 Proposed Method

From Table 1, we notably remark that in the Arabic language, the correlation between ROUGE-2 and Overall Responsiveness is very low. In addition, almost no correlation exists between MeMoG, AutoSummENG, NPowER and Overall Responsiveness for the Arabic language. Perhaps, this is due to the complexity of the Arabic language structure. For the English language, we note that the correlation between automatic metrics and Overall Responsiveness is better than for the Arabic language but it still low. This motivated us to combine those automatic metrics in order to predict Overall Responsiveness. So, the combination of those metrics will give better correlation. In addition, the Overall Responsiveness score is a real number between 1 and 5 which assesses the content and the linguistic quality of a text summary. This means that we should combine multiple features related to the content and the linguistic quality of a summary. For this reason we have added multiple syntactic features. Then, a predictive model for each language is built by combining multiple features.

The basic idea of the proposed evaluation methodology is based on the prediction of the human grade score (Overall Responsiveness) (Dang and Karolina, 2008) for a candidate summary in Arabic or English languages. This prediction is obtained by the extraction of features from the candidate summary itself, from comparing the candidate summary with the source documents or with reference summaries. To obtain the predictive model for each language, extracted features are combined using a linear regression algorithm. In the following subsections, we will first give the list of used features, then we move to the description of the combination scheme.

3.1 Used features

In the proposed method we use several classes of features that are related to the content and the linguistic quality of a text summary. The list of used

Table 1: Kendall's Tau Correlation Between Gradings (R2, MeMoG, AutoSummENG, NPowER and OR) with p-value < 0.1 from MultiLing 2013 corpus

Language	R2 to OR	MeMoG* to OR	AutoSummENG* to OR	NPowER* to OR
Arabic	0.125	0.018	0.029	0.031
English	0.216	0.202	0.239	0.234

* we give the kendall correlation for MeMoG, AutoSummENG and NPowER with parameters: minimum length of N-grams = maximum length of N-grams = window size=3

features are:

- ROUGE Scores: ROUGE scores are designed to evaluate the content of a text summary. They are based on the overlap of words N-grams between a candidate summary and one or more reference summaries. According to (Conroy and Dang, 2008), ROUGE variants which take into account large contexts may capture the linguistic qualities of the summary such as some grammatical phenomena. We mean that ROUGE variants that use bigrams, trigrams or more can capture some grammatical phenomena from the well formation of reference sentences. For this reason, we include ROUGE scores which take into account large contexts in the ROUGE feature class:ROUGE-1 (R1), ROUGE-2 (R2), ROUGE-3 (R3), ROUGE-4 (R4) and ROUGE-5 (R5) which calculate respectively words overlaps of bigrams, trigrams, 4-grams and 5-grams.
- AutoSummENG, MeMoG and NPowER scores: Those three scores are based on N-grams graph (Giannakopoulos and Karkaletsis, 2010) are used to assess the content and the readability of a summary. To calculate these scores, we should adjust three parameters: minimum length of N-grams, maximum length of N-grams and window size between two N-grams. In our experiments, we have used three configurations for each score. The first configuration gives 1 to minimum length of N-gram, 2 to maximum length of N-gram and 3 to window size. The second configuration assigns 3 to minimum length of N-gram, 3 to maximum length of N-gram and 3 to window size. Finally, the third one attributs 4 to minimum length of N-gram, 4 to maximum length of N-gram and 3 to window size. In fact, because Overall responsivness scores evaluate the content and the linguistic quality of summary, we have chosen the first configuration to assess the content and the two other configurations to capture some grammatical phenomena from the well formation of reference sentences. We have assumed that also for those scores configurations which take into account large contexts may capture the linguistic qualities of the summary.
- SIMetrix scores: we have used the following six scores calculated by SIMetrix (Louis and Nenkova, 2013) : the Kullback-Leibler (KL) divergence between the source documents (SDs) and the candidate summary (CS) (KLInputSummary), the KL divergence between the CS and the SDs (KLSummaryInput), the unsmoothed version of Jensen Shannon divergence between the SDs and the CS (unsmoothedJSD) and the smoothed one (smoothedJSD), the probability of uni-grams of the CS given SDs (unigramProb), multinomial probability of the CS given SDs (multinomialProb).
- Syntactic features: the syntactic structure of sentences is an important factor that can determine the linguistic quality of texts. (Schwarm and Ostendorf, 2005) and (Feng et al., 2010) used syntactic features to gauge the readability of text as assessment of reading level. While (Kate et al., 2010) used syntactic features to predict linguistic quality of natural-language documents. We implement some of these features using the Stanford parser (Klein and Manning, 2003). We calculate the number and the average number of noun phrases (NP), verbal phrases (VP) and prepositional phrases (PP). The average number of each of the previous phrases is calculated as the ratio between the number of one of the previous phrase type and the total number of sentences.

3.2 Combination scheme

Before building a predictive model, we should first calculate the values of all the features.

Then, We select the relevant ones using "wrapper method"(Kohavi and John, 1997). This method evaluates subsets of features which allows to detect the possible interactions between features. It evaluates the performance of each subset of features, then it gives as a result the best one. This does not mean that the other features are not good, but it means that the combination of features from the best subset gives the best performance.

Now, to build the predictive model (combination scheme) for a language, we have used several basic (single algorithms) and "ensemble learning" algorithms, implemented by the Weka environment (Witten et al., 2011), using a regression method. For basic algorithms we use "GaussianProcesses", LinearRegression and SMOReg. For "ensemble learning" algorithms, we use "Bagging" (Breiman, 1996), "AdditiveRegression"(Friedman, 1999), "Stacking" (Wolpert, 1992) and "Vote" (Kuncheva, 2004).

After testing the algorithms, we adopt the one that produces the best predictive model. The validation of each model is performed by two methods: cross-validation method with 10 folds and supplied test set method.

4 Evaluation

4.1 Corpus

In this article, we use the TAC 2011 MultiLing Pilot 2011 corpus (Giannakopoulos et al., 2011) and the MultiLing 2013 corpus (Giannakopoulos, 2013). The two corpus involve the source documents, peer summaries, model summaries and automatic and manual evaluation results. The first corpus is available in 7 languages. We use only the Arabic and English documents. For Arabic languages, there are seven participating systems and two baseline systems. While for English language, there are eight participating systems and two baseline systems. For each language, source documents are divided to ten collections of newspaper articles. Each collection includes ten articles related to the same topic. Each collection has three model (human) summaries. Each summarization system is invited to generate a summary for each collection of documents. For MultiLing 2013 corpus, This corpus is available in 10 languages. We use only the Arabic and English documents. For each collection, there are eight participating systems, two baseline systems and 15 collections of newspaper articles. Each collection includes ten articles related to the same topic. Each summarization system is invited to generate a summary for each collection.

4.2 Experiments and results

We have experimented our method in summary level evaluation (Micro-evaluation). At this level, we take, for each Summarizer system, each produced summary in a separate entry. It is worth mentioning that this evaluation level is more difficult than system level evaluation (i.e. where the average quality of a summarizing system is measured) even for MonoLingual summary evaluation (Ellouze et al., 2013), (Ellouze et al., 2016). For each language, we have tested several single and "ensemble learning" classifiers integrated on Weka environment and based on regression method like GaussianProcesses, linearRegression, vote, Bagging, etc.

We validate our models using cross-validation with 10 folds and using supplied test set. For cross-validation method, we have calculated the features from "MultiLing 2013" corpus. While, for supplied test set method we have used "MultiLing 2013" corpus as training set and "MultiLing Pilot TAC'2011" corpus as testing set. We have chosen to train our models on "MultiLing 2013" corpus because we have more summaries in this corpus (150 summaries for Arabic and 149 for English). To evaluate the proposed method, we study the correlation of Pearson (Pearson, 1895), Spearman (Spearman, 1910) and Kendall (Kendall, 1938) between the manual scores (Overall Responsiveness) and the scores produced by the proposed method. Furthermore, we report the "Root Mean Squared Error" (RMSE) measure generated by each model. This measure is based on the difference between the manual scores (Overall responsiveness) and the predicted scores.

Arabic Summary Evaluation

We begin with the experiments performed with Arabic language. The selected features for Arabic models are: autosummeng$_{443}$, unsmoothed-JSD, unigramProb, multinomialProb, ROUGE-3 and number of NP phrases in the summary. The Pearson, the Spearman and the Kendall Correlations and the root mean square error (RMSE) generated by each classifier for Arabic language are presented in Table 2.

Table 2 shows the performance of the selected features in building the predictive models using

Table 2: Pearson, Spearman and Kendall Correlations with Overall Responsiveness and RMSE (between brackets) for Various Single and Ensemble learning Classifiers for Arabic language

Classifiers	**Cross-validation**				**Supplied test set**			
Single classifiers								
	Peason	Spearman	Kendall	RMSE	Peason	Spearman	Kendall	RMSE
GaussianProcesses	0.329	0.328	0.236	**0.696**	**0.224**	0.229	0.163	**0.591**
LinearRegression	0.306	0.292	0.207	0.708	0.196	0.197	0.148	0.647
SMOReg	0.299	0.304	0.216	0.711	0.128	0.181	0.142	0.632
"Ensemble learning" classifiers								
AdditiveRegression	**0.337**	0.327	0.232	0.697	0.185	0.194	0.150	0.643
Vote	0.320	0.330	0.236	0.705	0.212	0.226	0.169	0.650
Bagging	0.330	**0.335**	**0.239**	0.700	0.185	0.218	0.160	0.637
Stacking	0.308	0.322	0.228	0.701	0.217	**0.232**	**0.172**	0.625

several single and ensemble learning classifiers. In the case of cross validation method, the results show that the model built from the "ensemble learning" classifier "Bagging" produced the best Kendall (0.239) and Spearman (0.335) correlations, "AdditiveRegression" produced the best Pearson (0.337) correlation while the "GaussianProcesses" have produced the lowest RMSE (0.696). In the case of supplied test set method, Table 2 indicates that the best "ensemble learning" classifier is the "Stacking" which provides a model having a Kendall correlation of 0.171 and a Spearman correlation of (0.232) while the "GaussianProcesses" have produced the best Pearson (0.224) correlation and the lowest RMSE. Another notable observation is that the correlation using cross-validation is more important than using supplied test set. Whereas, the RMSE using supplied test set is lower than using cross-validation. This means that the error between the predictive values and the actual values is less important using supplied test set. The decrease of correlation between the cross-validation method and the supplied test set method needs to be studied further in future works.

We pass now to the comparison between the performance of the best obtained model and the baseline metrics that were adopted by the MultiLing workshop such as R-2, MeMoG and also we add the best variant of each of the three other famous metrics AutoSummENG, NPoWER and SIMetrix. Table 3 details the different correlations and RMSEs of baseline metrics and our different experimentations.

From Table 3, the model built from the combination of selected features has the best correlation and RMSE comparing to baselines. When observing the Table 3, we see the gap between baseline metrics and the model build from selected features. In addition, we notice the decrease of correlation on both methods of validation (cross-validation, supplied test set), when we tried to remove one of the classes of features. Moreover, we remark that removing SIMetrix metric from the selected features have a big effect on its correlation with Overall Responsiveness when using supplied test set as validation method.

Besides, we note that the correlation of the best model with Overall Responsiveness is low, while it is more important than the correlation of baselines. This may be due to the small set of the observations per Arabic language. We need a larger set of observations to determine the best combination of features and to have better correlation. Furthermore, perhaps, this is due to the complexity of the Arabic language structure which is an agglutinative language where agglutination (Grefenstette et al., 2005) occurs when articles, prepositions and conjunctions are attached to the beginning of words and pronouns are attached to the end of words. This phenomenon can greatly influence the operation of comparing the candidate summary with reference summaries. Especially when a word appears in the candidate summary without agglutination while it appears in a reference summary in an agglutinative form and vice versa.

English Summary Evaluation

We pass now to the different experiments performed with English language. The selected features for English models are NPowER_{123}, autosummeng_{443}, the number of NP phrases in the text summary, the average number of PP per sentence in a text summary. The Pearson, the Spearman and the Kendall Correlations and the root-mean-square error (RMSE) generated by each

Table 3: Pearson, Spearman and Kendall Correlations with Overall Responsiveness Score and RMSE (between brackets) for Arabic language

Baselines			
Score	Peason	Spearman	Kendall
ROUGE-2	0.164	0.175	0.125
$AutoSummENG_{443}$	0.055	0.063	0.045
$MeMoG_{443}$	0.066	0.039	0.03
$NPowER_{443}$	0.063	0.064	0.049
SIMetrix_unigramProb	0.258	0.257	0.182

Our experimentations								
	Cross-validation				**Supplied test set**			
Score	Peason	Spearman	Kendall	RMSE	Peason	Spearman	Kendall	RMSE
Combining selected features (CSF)	**0.330**	**0.335**	**0.239**	0.700	**0.217**	**0.232**	**0.172**	0.625
CSF without ROUGE	0.276	0.298	0.213	0.713	0.194	0.149	0.107	0.638
CSF without AutoSummENG	0.315	0.319	0.227	0.704	0.190	0.225	0.160	0.647
CSF without SIMetrix	0.310	0.340	0.243	0.717	0.057	0.048	0.039	0.646
CSF without Synt Feat	0.285	0.244	0.172	0.708	0.199	0.154	0.111	**0.601**

classifier for English language are presented in Table 4.

Table 4 shows the performance of the selected features in building the predictive models using several single and ensemble learning classifiers for the English language. For cross validation method, the results show that the model built from the "ensemble learning" classifier "Bagging" produced the best Kendall (0.393), Spearman (0.537) and Pearson (0.529) correlations and the lowest RMSE (0.652).

For supplied test set validation method, Table 2 indicates that the best "ensemble learning" classifier in terms of correlation and RMSE is also the "Bagging". In fact, this "ensemble learning" has the best correlations (i.e. Kendall: 0.322) and the lowest RMSE (0.754). Again, we note that the correlation using cross-validation is more important than using supplied test set. The decrease of correlation between the cross-validation method and the supplied test set method can be caused by the variation of the human evaluator and/or the change of evaluation guidelines from MultiLing 2011 to MultiLing 2013.

We now move to the comparison between the performance of the best obtained model and the baseline metrics that were adopted by the MultiLing workshop such as ROUGE-2 and MeMoG and also we add the best variant of each of the three other famous metrics AutoSummENG, NPoWER and SIMetrix. Table 5 details the different correlations and RMSEs of baseline metrics, other famous metrics and our best model.

From Table 5, we see the gap between baseline metrics and our experiments, with both validation methods. We have retained the model built from the "Bagging" classifier with both validation methods. We observe also that the elimination of one of the used classes of features decreases the correlation of the best model (built from selected features) with Overall Responsiveness and increases the RMSE. Furthermore, we note that the elimination of syntactic features class decreases enormously the correlation with the use of both methods of validation. The surprising notification is that the elimination of AutoSummENG score increases the correlation instead of decreasing it. Generally, we have noted the effect of syntactic features in the best model for both languages (Arabic, English).

5 Conclusion

We have presented a method for evaluating the Overall Responsiveness of text summary in both Arabic and English language. This method is based on a combination of ROUGE scores, AutoSummENG scores, MeMoG scores, NPowER scores, SIMetrix scores and a variety of syntactic features. We have combined these features using a regression method. Before building the linear regression model, we select the relevant features using the "Wrapper subset evaluator" method. The selected method includes automatic metrics and syntactic features. And generally automatic features that take into account large context are selected ($autosummeng_{443}$, ROUGE-3, etc). This confirms the hypothesis of (Conroy and Dang, 2008) which indicates that the integration of con-

Table 4: Pearson, Spearman and Kendall Correlations with Overall Responsiveness and RMSE (between brackets) for Various Single and Ensemble learning Classifiers for English language

Classifiers	**Cross-validation**				**Supplied test set**			
	Single classifiers							
	Peason	Spearman	Kendall	RMSE	Peason	Spearman	Kendall	RMSE
GaussianProcesses	0.519	0.508	0.367	0.656	0.395	0.365	0.258	0.780
LinearRegression	0.514	0.490	0.353	0.658	0.236	0.384	0.277	1.542
SMOReg	0.510	0.5184	0.375	0.668	0.372	0.310	0.227	0.803
	"Ensemble learning" classifiers							
AdditiveRegression	0.522	0.499	0.360	1.092	0.276	0.427	0.313	3.028
Vote	0.523	0.522	0.380	0.661	0.232	0.395	0.285	1.475
Bagging	**0.529**	**0.537**	**0.393**	**0.652**	**0.465**	**0.444**	**0.322**	**0.754**
Stacking	0.503	0.519	0.379	0.663	0.372	0.427	0.304	0.837

Table 5: Pearson, Spearman and Kendall Correlations with Overall Responsiveness Score and RMSE (between brackets) for Arabic language

Baselines			
Score	Peason	Spearman	Kendall
ROUGE-2	0.314	0.316	0.216
$AutoSummENG_{123}$	0.358	0.385	0.263
$MeMoG_{123}$	0.370	0.362	0.254
$NPowER_{123}$	0.385	0.386	0.266
SIMetrix_unsmoothedJSD	0.235	0.248	0.173

Our experimentations								
	Cross-validation				**Supplied test set**			
Score	Peason	Spearman	Kendall	RMSE	Peason	Spearman	Kendall	RMSE
Combining selected features (CSF)	**0.529**	**0.537**	**0.393**	**0.652**	**0.465**	**0.444**	**0.322**	**0.754**
CSF without AutoSummENG	0.466	0.459	0.333	0.680	*0.502*	*0.452*	*0.335*	0.802
CSF without NPowER	0.505	0.498	0.363	0.663	0.310	0.285	0.203	0.794
CSF without Synt Feat	0.396	0.388	0.267	0.705	0.377	0.312	0.236	0.834

tent scores which take into account large context may captivate some grammatical phenomena.

To evaluate our method, we have compared the correlation of the best model (built with selected features) and of baselines with manual Overall Responsiveness.We have tested two methods of validation of predictive models : cross validation with 10 folds and supplied test set. The results show that, in both languages, the correlation of the best model with Overall Responsiveness is low, while it is more importante then the correlation of baselines. This may be due to the small set of the observations per language. We need a larger set of observations to determine the best combination of features and to have better correlation. Moreover, we note that the correlation using cross-validation is more important than using supplied test set. The decrease of correlation between the cross-validation method and the supplied test set method needs to be studied further in future works.

The main steps we plan to take in our future works, are the construction of predictive models for more languages and the addition of other types of features such as entities based features, part-of-speech features, Co-reference Features, shallow features, etc.

References

Leo Breiman. 1996. Bagging predictors. *Machine learning*, 24:123–140.

John M. Conroy and Hoa T. Dang. 2008. Mind the gap: Dangers of divorcing evaluations of summary content from linguistic quality. In *Proceedings of the 22nd International Conference on Computational Linguistics (Coling 2008)*, pages 145–152.

H. Trang Dang and Owczarzak. Karolina. 2008. Overview of the tac 2008 update summarization task. In *In TAC 2008 Workshop - Notebook papers and results*, pages 10–23.

Samira Ellouze, Maher Jaoua, and Lamia Hadrich Belguith. 2013. An evaluation summary method based on a combination of content and linguistic metrics. In *Proceedings of the International Conference Recent Advances in Natural Language Processing(RANLP)*, pages 245–251, Hissar, Bulgaria.

Samira Ellouze, Maher Jaoua, and Lamia Hadrich Belguith. 2016. Automatic evaluation of a summary's linguistic quality. In *Proceedings of Natural Language Processing and Information Systems (NLDB). Lecture Notes in Computer Science*, pages 392–400.

Lijun Feng, Martin Jansche, Matt Huenerfauth, and Nomie Elhadad. 2010. A Comparison of Features for Automatic Readability Assessment. In *Proceedings of the 23rd International Conference on Computational Linguistics (COLING 2010)*, pages 276–284.

Jerome H. Friedman. 1999. Stochastic gradient boosting. Technical report, Stanford University.

George Giannakopoulos and Vangelis Karkaletsis. 2010. Summarization system evaluation variations based on n-gram graphs. In *Proceedings of the Third Text Analysis Conference, TAC 2010*.

George Giannakopoulos and Vangelis Karkaletsis. 2013. Summary evaluation: Together we stand npower-ed. In *Proceedings of 14th international conference on Computational Linguistics and Intelligent Text Processing - Volume 2*, pages 436–450.

George Giannakopoulos, Vangelis Karkaletsis, George Vouros, and P. Stamatopoulos. 2008. Summarization system evaluation revisited: N-gram graphs. *ACM Transactions on Speech and Language Processing*, 5(3):1–39.

George Giannakopoulos, Mahmoud El-Haj, Benot Favre, Marianna Litvak, Josef Steinberger, and Vasudeva Varma. 2011. Tac 2011 multiling pilot overview. In *Proceedings of the Fourth Text Analysis Conference*.

George Giannakopoulos, Jeff Kubina, John M. Conroy, Josef Steinberger, Benot Favre, Mijail A. Kabadjov, Udo Kruschwitz, and Massimo Poesio. 2015. Multiling 2015: Multilingual summarization of single and multi-documents, on-linefora, and call-center conversations. In *Proceedings of the 16th Annual SIGdial Meeting on Discourse and Dialogue*.

George Giannakopoulos. 2013. Multi-document multilingual summarization and evaluation tracks in acl 2013 multiling workshop. In *Proceedings of the MultiLing 2013 Workshop on Multilingual Multi-document Summarization*.

Gregory Grefenstette, Nasredine Semmar, and Faïza Elkateb-Gara. 2005. Modifying a natural language processing system for european languages to treat arabic in information processing and information retrieval applications. In *Proceedings of the ACL Workshop on Computational Approaches to Semitic Languages*, pages 31–37.

Eduard Hovy, Chin-Yew Lin, Liang Zhou, and Junichi Fukumoto. 2006. Automated summarization evaluation with basic elements. In *Proceedings of the Fifth Conference on Language Resources and Evaluation (LREC)*.

Rohit J. Kate, Xiaoqiang Luo, Siddharth Patwardhan, Martin Franz, Radu Florian, Raymond J. Mooney, Salim Roukos, and Chris Welty. 2010. Learning to predict readability using diverse linguistic features. In *Proceedings of the 23rd International Conference on Computational Linguistics*, pages 546–554.

Maurice Kendall. 1938. A new measure of rank correlation. *Biometrika*, 30:81–89.

Dan Klein and Christopher D. Manning. 2003. Accurate unlexicalized parsing. In *Proceedings of the 41st Annual Meeting on Association for Computational Linguistics - Volume 1*, pages 423–430.

Ron Kohavi and George H. John. 1997. Wrappers for feature subset selection. *Artificial Intelligence*, 97(1-2):273–324.

Ludmila I. Kuncheva. 2004. *Combining Pattern Classifiers: Methods and Algorithms*. Wiley-Interscience.

Chin-Yew Lin and Eduard Hovy. 2003. Automatic evaluation of summaries using n-gram cooccurrence statistics. In *Proceedings of the 2003 Conference of the North American Chapter of the Association for Computational Linguistics on Human Language Technology - Volume 1*, pages 71–78.

Annie Louis and Ani Nenkova. 2013. Automatically assessing machine summary content without a gold standard. *Computational Linguistics*, 39(2):267–300, jun.

Karl Pearson. 1895. Mathematical contributions to the theory of evolution, ii: Skew variation in homogeneous material. *Philosophical Transactions of Royal Society London (A)*, 186:343–414.

Sarah E. Schwarm and Mari Ostendorf. 2005. Reading level assessment using support vector machines and statistical language models. In *Proceedings of the Annual Meeting of the Association for Computational Linguistics*, pages 523–530.

Charles Spearman. 1910. Correlation calculated from faulty data. *British Journal of Psychology*, 3:271–295.

Stephen Tratz and Eduard Hovy. 2008. Bewte: basic elements with transformations for evaluation. In *Proceedings of Text Analysis Conference (TAC) Workshop*.

Ian H. Witten, Eibe Frank, and Mark A. Hall. 2011. *Data Mining: Practical Machine Learning Tools and Techniques*. Morgan Kaufmann Publishers Inc., San Francisco, CA, USA, 3rd edition.

David H. Wolpert. 1992. Stacked generalization. *Neural Networks*, 5:241–259.

Author Index

Association for Computational Linguistics
209 N. Eighth Street
Stroudsburg, Pennsylvania 18360

ISBN 978-1-5108-3867-3

CURRAN ASSOCIATES INC.
proceedings.com